# BUSINESS AMPLIFIER

Find out how your intelligence can harness the best resources available.

José Motta Lopes

bAmpli.com

José Motta Lopes

# BUSINESS AMPLIFIER

2nd Edition – 2020
José Motta da Rocha Lopes
Rio de Janeiro

Copyright © 2020 José Motta Lopes

All rights reserved. Reproduction in whole or in part by any means or process is prohibited, including graphic, photographic, reprographic, video graphic, eBook, and Internet systems.

The Author believes that the information presented here is correct. However, there is no guarantee, express or implied, that the use of such information will lead to the desired result. Any errata will be available for reference on the website listed below.

Trademarks, acronyms and terms mentioned and recognized as trademarks are the property of their respective owners.

# bAmpli.com

Cover: Ricardo Bergara

Revision 2.0 - English

Copyright © 2020 José Motta Lopes

All rights reserved.

ISBN-979-86-029496-3-6

# ACKNOWLEDGMENT

This book has matured for twenty years. In the 1990s, after a Theory of Constraints workshop, a student approached me asking: What else do you have to offer on this subject? Apart from consulting, very little, I answered bleakly.

At that time, the task of developing a custom information system would require a huge amount of human resources. Software tools were rudimentary and micro computers were more expensive compared to what we have today. Micros are now great and open source brings to life great knowledge intensive workflows. I thank those who kept reminding me to improve my response.

The time passed, the step was taken and the book is ready! I thank my brother Ricardo Motta Lopes for the support and encouragement to this endeavor. I also thank the qualified review by Rosaura Morais, Marcelo Rangel and my son Tiago, questioning and warning about important points to consider. Thanks also to Ricardo Bergara for the cover art.

# Table of Contents

Introduction ............................................................................................. 1

20's: The starting point is the invention of the factory ................... 3

   *Cost Accounting* ................................................................................ 4

   *Wars distort the CA* .......................................................................... 6

      Measure #1 is Cost Reduction ....................................................... 7

50's: Deming introduces SPC in Japan ............................................. 11

   *Deming Principles on the Return to America* ................................ 13

   *Statistical Process Control (SPC)* .................................................... 14

      Control Charts ............................................................................. 16

      The Deming Process .................................................................... 18

   *Total Productive Maintenance (TPM)* ............................................ 20

      Company Global Performance .................................................... 21

   *Just in Time (JIT)* ............................................................................. 26

      Measure #1 is Return on Investment ........................................... 27

80's: The West Turn Over .................................................................. 33

   *Theory of Constraints (TOC)* ......................................................... 37

      Measure #1 is the Gain ................................................................ 39

      Constraint determines performance ............................................ 41

      Decision Process .......................................................................... 44

   *P&Q Factory* ................................................................................... 46

      How much profit does the P&Q Factory? .................................... 48

10's: Life goes on ................................................................................ 55

   *The goal is the great global* ........................................................... 55

   *The sum of the local optima almost always takes us away from the global optimum* ............................................................................... 57

**The Conflict in the Pyramid** ........................................... 59
   *Pyramid Expands Control* .......................................... 60
   *Manager cycle* ......................................................... 61
   *Pyramid Distorts Information/Decisions* ................. 63
   *The conflict in the pyramid* .................................... 65
      Conflict Analysis ................................................... 66
   *Measures evolution* ................................................. 67
   *Ampli Business* ......................................................... 69

**Process Cycle** ............................................................... 71
   *P&Q Overseas* ........................................................... 74
      P&Q Distribution ................................................... 76
      P&Q Commerce ...................................................... 77
      P&Q Services ......................................................... 78
      Interconnected Cycles ........................................ 80
   *Project Guide* ........................................................... 82
   *Niche markets* .......................................................... 87

**Times of Gain** .............................................................. 91
   *Normal distribution* ................................................. 91
   *Process Spin* ............................................................. 94

**Cyclo: Gain Machine** ................................................ 97
   *Cyclo Operations* ..................................................... 99

**bAmpli: Business Amplifier** .................................... 101
   *Plan x Reality* .......................................................... 102
   *bAmpli Gain* ............................................................. 103
   *Return on investment* ............................................ 105

**Business Circuits** ..................................................... 107

**Ampli Business** ..................................................................... **109**

    *Layers are the solution* ................................................. *109*

    *Layer 1 - Company Indicators* ...................................... *111*

    *Layer 2 - Cyclo: Gain Machine* ..................................... *113*

    *Layer 3 - bAmpli: Business Amplifier* ........................... *115*

    *Layer 4 - bAmpli Business Circuit* ................................ *117*

**Conclusion** ............................................................................ **121**

**About the author** ................................................................. **123**

**Glossary** ............................................................................... **125**

**Bibliography** ........................................................................ **129**

JOSÉ MOTTA LOPES

# Introduction

This book was written thinking of all those who need to make decisions in their work environment. A company is an organization traditionally viewed as a set of individual operations, where each has an obligation to optimize the sector under its responsibility. However, everyone's goal should be to progress continuously and collectively toward the global optimum.

A process of continuous improvement is always a successful process of continuous change. We know how difficult it is to manage, discuss, deploy and measure the impact of a change on company goals. How to establish a professional and systematic process of continuous change? How do you know if the proposed modification will actually improve the process or make things look better from a certain angle, making the whole worse?

In responding to such vital questions, thinkers around the world have developed management philosophies that make it possible to maximize man's ability to work together intelligently and wisely, overcoming natural limitations.

How has human intelligence better leveraged our available resources? This is what this reading expects to provide.

JOSÉ MOTTA LOPES

## 20's: The starting point is the invention of the factory

Henry Ford invented the dream factory that hit the middle-class families eager to buy their first car. With unbeatable quality and price, the Ford Model T showed the world how to boost industrial production volume. The new factory design was based on a production line that moved material between fixed stations, where workers performed specific assembly tasks. Until products finally emerged at the end of the production line, it was necessary to devise and execute a profound transformation in industrial production at the time.

While inventing the factory of the modern era, Henry Ford did not know if man would adapt well to repetitive work, being obliged to always do the same thing all the time. He thought himself too creative and unable to work in production positions. In 1922, in the book "My Life and Work", he said he was terrified, just thinking about the idea. Employee career advancement began in class C and evolved into classes B and A. In addition, creative minds would build the tools and oversee production, meaning they would invent the factory along with it. Since everything was new, there was a profound shortage of artists in industry and industrial methods, both from the producer's and the product's point of view. Much would still be invented and reinvented in the years to come, but the conceptual step was taken.

Not only in Chaplin's films was there concern that repetitive work might somehow hurt the worker. Much research has been done to ensure that using the same set of muscles for eight hours would not cause sequelae to the human body. In January 1914, the policy of not refusing workers on account of their physical condition, except contagious diseases, was instituted. According to Henry Ford's own account, training to make the employee proficient lasted one day in 43% of cases; to 42% could last up to two weeks; 14% could last from one month to one year; with 1% would spend from 1 to 6 years. Nowadays, jobs require much more intensive knowledge.

In the era of the Model T, Ford factory management considered ONE factory and ONE product being produced. The accounts were relatively simple: add all expenses and divide by the number of cars to get the unit cost. Add the profit that rewards the investments, and the price of the product was obtained. Better than that, the factory was reinventing itself every day and optimizing production costs, resulting in a virtuous spiral.

## *Cost Accounting*

General Motors, Ford's main competitor, had no capital to wage a price war. This strategy would not take the Model T from the top of the market. The chosen action, under the command of Alfred Sloan, was to offer not cheaper cars, but a wider range of better quality cars.

He bet that a good portion of consumers would like to have an option besides basic transportation when changing their first car. GM's competent staff also came to the conclusion that "best quality" should not translate into complex engineering solutions. At the time, technical innovations were expensive, required long development times and had unpredictable results, meaning they were difficult to write off.

Decision made in 1923, a 9-year-old Chevrolet gained aesthetic innovations that gave it the appearance of a handcrafted luxury car. The blockbuster showed the direction that would later inspire the integration of brands like Pontiac, Oldsmobile, Buick, and Cadillac into a shared parts scheme and lacquered paint that combined varied colors and drying time as fast as Ford's black paint. Focusing on car styling, GM sales surpassed Ford's in 1927, when the Model T was discontinued because of poor sales. From then on, GM would stay ahead virtually all the time.

However, to switch the strategy and offer cars of varying models and colors, GM had to review the factory management calculations. It still had ONE factory but now it produced SEVERAL products. You could not just add all expenses and divide by the number of cars to get the cost of the product. It would be necessary to change the administration to deal with several models assembled from shared parts. Complicated!

To model ONE company that produced VARIOUS products, each product was accounted for separately. This separation required identifying and grouping the accounting entries for income and expense, according to the model / product color combination. Company revenue was obtained by summing the Sales of each Product. To get the company's profit, subtract from that revenue the costs of raw materials, labor costs and overhead which included the other fixed costs of the company. Cost Accounting was then created and the company's net profit equation was as follows:

**COMPANY INDICATORS**

NP = (PS - RM - WF) - OH

    NP    Net Profit
    PS    Product Sales
    RM    Raw Material
    WF    Workforce
    OH    Overhead

Since workers earned by production at the beginning of the century, the profit formula had three terms proportional to production, namely variables: revenue from product sales, raw material and labor costs. As at Ford's original factory, only Overhead computed the company's fixed costs.

## *Wars distort the CA*

Cost Accounting (CA) was a vital tool in exploiting the weakness of the Ford Model T. It was also vital throughout the rest of the twentieth century, equipping each company and being widespread worldwide. Cost Accounting has managed and conquered challenges in two world wars, being used to this day by managers, investors, market officials and the entire organized corporate civilization.

In the 1920s, workers earned per piece produced. This means that Raw Material and Labor were accounted for as variable cost, i.e. most expenses were proportional to production. Later, in the 1940s, workers would receive a fixed salary, regardless of production. From then on, the Labor Force was accounted for as a fixed cost. Updating the company's net profit calculation:

NP = (PS - RM) - (WF + OH)

In the updated Profit formula, only Product Sales revenue and Raw Material costs are proportional to production. The more the company's production is sold, the higher these values are. Without production and sales, both are zero.

Labor and Overhead together represent the company's Operating Expense, closely associated with its existence. If the company has idle capacity and production increases, the Operating Expense does not increase. However, if the company's output declines, or even produces nothing, Labor and Overhead costs remain there, firm and strong.

## Measure #1 is Cost Reduction

Looking at the Profit formula, we find that virtually all of its terms are costs, except Product Sales. Costs also represent the vast majority of the company's accounting entries. Throughout the world, for much of the twentieth century, cost savings were the main factor influencing the decision of investors and managers to increase the company's profit. Cost reduction was considered Measure #1 because Cost Accounting dictated the rules of business management.

In addition to Profit, Cost Accounting has always tried to extract other indicators that would allow us to evaluate the performance of the company and its respective products. However, see in the chart below that the fundamentals of Cost Accounting have been shaken over time.

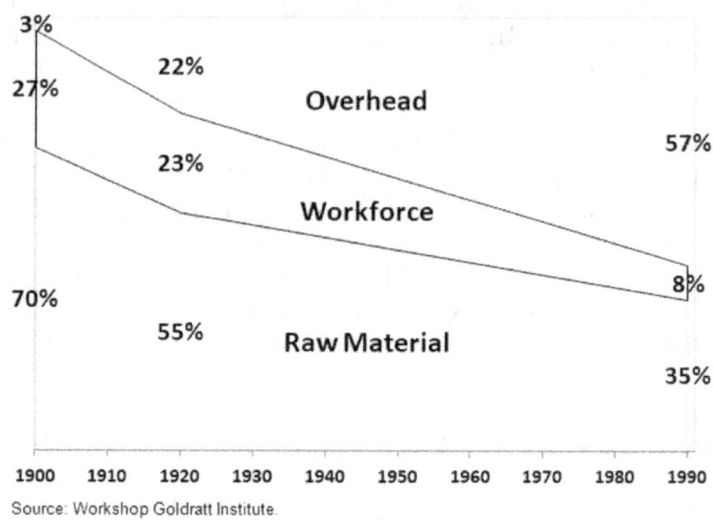

Source: Workshop Goldratt Institute.

Labor moved to the side of fixed costs in the 1940s. Overhead jumped from 3% of the total in 1900 to 60% of costs by the end of the century.

With so much variation, how would managers measure product performance? How would you decide how much of each product to make to maximize the company's profit? For a long time, an ideal formula that represented the "cost of the product" was sought. Would it be possible to create a magical imaginary measure that would guide managers and investors in their analysis and decisions?

For nearly the entire twentieth century, Cost Accounting specialists have tried to spread the fixed cost across each of the company´s products. As a result, different criteria emerged that attempted to create fictitious measures to represent the "cost of the product". The great difficulty is that the criteria were constantly overwhelmed by the reality of the facts.

It was a long time before everyone was convinced that there is no point in talking about the cost or profit of a product. Yes, the company has a Profit.

JOSÉ MOTTA LOPES

## 50's: Deming introduces SPC in Japan

US professor William Edwards Deming, an electronics engineer with a doctorate in mathematics, was responsible for the statistical analysis of the 1939 US census. He worked at the Department of Agriculture, where he met Walter A. Shewhart, considered the father of Statistical Process Control (SPC). His ideas would greatly influence the future management theory that would be formulated by Deming.

During World War II, Deming applied his statistical knowledge to improving US production, teaching workers statistical process control. Despite their relative success, in a few years these methods would fall into disuse. In 1945, the atomic bombs dropped on Hiroshima and Nagasaki precipitated Japan's surrender to the Allied forces, and World War II was thus over. In 1947, the Allied Forces occupied Japan, and the US government called Deming to assist in the Japanese census. His involvement with Japanese society eventually generated an invitation from the Union of Engineers and Scientists of Japan (JUSE). They had studied Shewhart's concepts and needed a statistics teacher to coordinate quality control seminars and lectures.

In 1950, Deming trained hundreds of Japanese engineers, managers and students. Deming's message to everyone was that improving quality would lower expenses, increase productivity and open new markets for products. Japanese industries applied their techniques and witnessed unprecedented production volumes. Deming refused to receive royalties for his work, but improvements in quality combined with lower costs created unprecedented international demand for Japanese products.

National Quality Awards were first instituted in the world in 1951, when the Deming Quality Award, created in Japan, had a major influence on the development and management of Japanese companies. In the United States, in 1956, Deming received the Shewhart Medal from the American Society for Quality Control. Only in 1959 would the first North American award be created: the Edward Medal.

Deming's contribution was so significant that the Emperor of Japan awarded him the Medal of the Second Order of the Sacred Treasury in 1960. In the 1980s, Deming was again honored in the United States, with honorary doctorate awards and awards for his name. In 1987, the Malcom Baldrige Award was created in the United States, based on current criteria that characterize quality management. From 1995, the Japanese Deming Prize ceases to exist, to make way for a World Prize.

Despite Deming's initial attempts to persuade the US industry in the 1940s, the Western industry would not pay due attention until much later in the 1980s. An NBC television program had to ask: "If Japan can ... Why can't we?", so that an avalanche of human and financial resources flooded the consulting market, with internal and external experts forming teams in pursuit of discipline for improving industrial processes. It was urgent to catch up and introduce Statistical Process Control (SPC), Just in Time (JIT), and Total Productive Maintenance (TPM), all techniques that originated in the eastern industry.

## *Deming Principles on the Return to America*

Back in the United States, Deming continued his consulting business and concluded that the US management philosophy would have to change to avoid the already declining industry. He then devoted himself to explaining the transformations that should occur to reverse this trend.

He emphasized that transformation could only be accomplished by man, not machines. Not only would their best efforts suffice to improve quality and productivity. Individual dedication, while essential, would not lead to success but to chaos, with a dispersion of knowledge and effort. Lead-oriented teamwork with principles-based knowledge needed to be done. These principles had already been successfully used in Japan in the 1950s and could be applied without distinction to organizations of all sizes, both in industry and services. In the classic book "Out of the Crisis," he presents the 14 principles for transforming Western administration.

At the flaps of the Brazilian edition, entitled "Quality: The Management Revolution", Noel Phillips, CEO of Autolatina and Edson Musa of Rhodia, underscore the importance of the transformations that occurred during the 1980s in their companies. Musa quotes: "By the end of '85, I realized that it was necessary to rethink the management paths of our company... then came the contact with Deming and his management philosophy. Fundamentally, what struck us most was the profound understanding that without improving processes, there are no permanent improvements that have no consequences, sometimes disastrous, in non-target locations". Phillips firmly states that "some of Dr. Deming's 14 points are a surprise and contrary to what is practiced by most Western companies".

## *Statistical Process Control (SPC)*

Globally known by the acronym SPC, Statistical Process Control was implemented in the West long after the eastern countries. The Japanese had been at the forefront since 1950, improving inputs and establishing long-term relationships with their suppliers based on loyalty and trust. In this way, suppliers became partners in the business, offering ever-better quality, ever greater savings, and everyone was winning.

On the western side, uncertainty about quality and timeliness led to the hiring of two or three suppliers, hoping that one of them would meet expectations. By this time, Japanese companies had already massively adhered to the Just in Time (JIT) delivery system. Time was saved because each supplier took parts directly to their customer's assembly line workstation. There was no need for inspection or material counting, reducing inventory and floor space. The obsession with quality control meant that 1% rejects and scrap rates were regularly maintained. The JIT discipline kept the process under control with predictable quality, quantity and regularity.

Toyota, inventor of Just in Time, bought from contract suppliers about 75 percent of its need for stamped parts. The rest was produced internally at the automaker. In the United States, at the same time, the opposite was true, that is, only 25% of the parts were purchased from suppliers. There was considerable difficulty in justifying Deming's proposed changes, as the new management philosophy would require training, that is, investments in education that would not be accounted for in companies' tangible net worth. There was a general resistance to knowledge, although advances required intensive knowledge. How to introduce new concepts if there was suspicion as to their effectiveness? How much would it cost? When would there be a return? What is the destination of those who try to embark on the trip?

The transformation would require teamwork from Western companies, but their assessment methods were individual. Those who worked helping others could pay dearly by having their own production impaired. Misperceptions of performance evaluation led to low team spirit, fostering rivalry, demotivation, frustration, depression, and inability to work. They were natural reactions to the outcome of evaluations that attributed to members of a group differences due to the system in which they worked. People's attempt at motivation rewarded those who did well within the system. However, it did not reward attempts to improve the system. The deterioration of teamwork exacerbated individual personalities, damaging the company. How to demand cooperation between different areas if everyone's aspiration was not to serve the company but to obtain a good evaluation? Managers and their subordinates should work for the company's progress.

Cost Accounting, allied up to that point in decision making, became an element of resistance to change. The clear advantages of having reduced inventory did not cheer up manufacturing and sales staff, as managers feared a lack of parts and preferred to have more inventory on hand. Sales could be lost if the customer could not wait. To negotiate better discounts, buyers were encouraged to buy large quantities of raw materials. Individual quotas of production, originating in accounting costs, were incompatible with **continuous improvement** or **kaizen**, so fundamental as a concept of Japanese culture that is expressed in one word only.

Deming warned of problems stemming from the excessive influence of Cost Accounting and treated them as deadly diseases. At the close of quarters, balance sheet distortions encouraged short-term profits, forcing managers to dispatch everything to the detriment of quality. Similarly, material and equipment expenses were extended and cuts in education and training fattened quarterly dividends. On the other hand, Japanese companies did not seem obligated to artificially maximize their profits to benefit shareholders. Big business was directed primarily at employees, and since they were benefited, to the detriment of profits, trust between management and the workforce arose naturally. By doing so, Oriental companies became world leaders in their categories by offering good products. As a result, profit became a natural consequence.

## Control Charts

With the consumer as the main link in the production line, Deming revolutionized the ineffective and costly mass inspection routines at the time. It stated that simple routine inspections did not improve, incorporate or guarantee product quality. Good or bad, the quality was already in the product, he emphasized. In contrast, it suggested that small samples of the product be inspected using control charts that provided customers and suppliers with a common language based on statistical control.

Deming laid the foundation for measurements using **operational definitions**. Taught at the time in colleges of letters and philosophy but almost never in business or engineering schools, the operational definition gives communicable meaning to a concept.

Adjectives such as good, reliable, warm, smooth, safe or insecure have no communicable meaning until they are expressed in operational terms of sampling, testing, and criteria. You can specify physical quantities, such as weight, diameter, color, pressure, temperature, among others. It may also refer to performance, eg. speed below 60 Km/h.

It is crucial that the operational definition has unanimous meaning in the market. It needs to be stable and time resistant, although it can be reviewed and updated. Statistically defined concepts include sampling, calculation, and interpretation of estimates and margins of uncertainty.

By introducing statistics into factories, inspired by Shewhart's concepts, Deming helped determine whether the origin of production problems was in **Common Causes** or **Special Causes**. This was crucial to the continuous improvement of industrial processes since it guided management in changing systems rather than in circles looking for culprits in production breakdowns and failures.

To show the difference, Deming explained that a stable process with no indication of a special cause of variation is considered **under statistical control**. It is a process whose variations are random but nevertheless its behavior in the near future is predictable.

See following an example of a typical **Control Chart**, where measurement samples are within safe limits, indicating normal process. Each possible failure is detected through an out-of-range sample sequence. The alarm is triggered, correction is enabled and quality returns to the process quickly.

### Control Chart

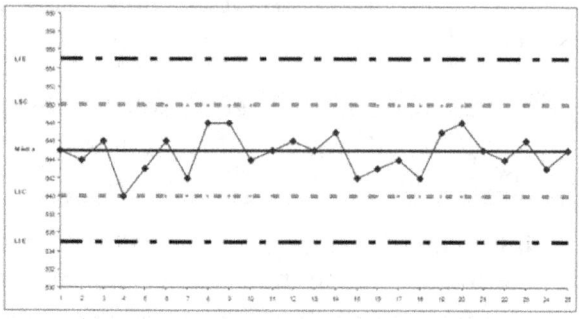

Source: Utilization of PDCA Cycle for Logistical Process Analysis. Joana França de Alencar.

Nothing prevents a sudden change from taking the process out of statistical control. If a special cause arises, it must be identified, treated and removed. As obvious special causes are detected and eliminated one by one, quality stabilizes.

You then reach a stable level of quality, as in the previous chart, in the presence of common causes only. But if eventually this quality is not yet acceptable, what to do? Focusing on eliminating the ups and downs of variations in a stable system can make the situation worse, creating additional disturbing variations. At this point, the only solution is process improvement, the sole responsibility of management. The causes of system failures are therefore called Common Causes and the causes of transient event failures are called Special Causes. Most of the problems are in the systems, Deming said, are the responsibility of management.

## The Deming Process

Deming's action plan foresaw management initiatives to transform the company. To implement the new philosophy, seminars were held involving a significant number of people. They should be aware of the need for transformation and the involvement of all in their principles. According to Deming, every activity and every task would be part of a process:

The Process would be divided into stages; the work would enter a certain stage, change state and continue, having as client the next stage. The final step would be for the user, buyer of the product or service. At each stage there would be production, that is, something would happen in the assets that enter the stage, causing its exit in a different state.

This Process definition, forged by Deming two world wars after the original Ford factory version, incorporates statistics into the working tools. The company is solely responsible for creating and developing a Process that meets the following requirements and rules:

## PROCESS

### Step 1 ▶ Step 2 ▶ ... ▶ Consumer

1. The process is divided into Steps;
2. The work enters a Step, changes state, and proceeds with the next Step as a client.
3. At each Step there is production, that is, something happens in the set of assets that enter a Step, causing their exit in a different state.
4. Each Step incorporates continual improvement of methods and procedures to meet subsequent Steps.
5. Each Step cooperates with the next and the previous, seeking optimization.
6. The Steps establish long-term trust relationships, such as: this is what I can do for you; here's what you can do for me.
7. The final Step is for the consumer, purchaser of the product or service.

8. The Steps work together, aiming at quality and customer satisfaction.
9. Consumer is the main link of the production line.

Step division is designed and executed according to the skills and workflow required by the Process.

Rule four includes the concept introduced by Deming in which Steps participate in a process of continuous improvement, or kaizen. To this end, among other responsibilities, and with the assistance of the SPC, management shall establish operational definitions related to the Process, perform sampling, measurements and eventually construct control charts that assess the quality of production.

## *Total Productive Maintenance (TPM)*

*"Following World War II, the Japanese industrial sectors borrowed and modified management and manufacturing skills and techniques from the United States."*

This is how Seiichi Nakajima defines Japanese-American cooperation in the second chapter of his book "Introduction to TPM". To this day, the whole world is celebrating this memorable postwar recovery effort in which the great global has been so objectively pursued.

Nakajima studied US preventive maintenance (PM) in 1950. He spent two decades visiting industries in America and Europe, observing western PM systems. Based on these observations, he developed Total Productive Maintenance (TPM) and launched it in Japan in 1971. At that time, only preventive maintenance was used in Japan. In the 1980s, it was replaced by predictive maintenance, which used monitoring and analysis techniques to diagnose equipment condition during operation, identifying signs of impending deterioration or failure.

TPM consists of a systematic, three-year program for enterprise development and implementation. It addresses maintenance by optimizing equipment effectiveness, eliminating production breakdowns and promoting product quality improvement through day-to-day workforce activities. By the late 1980s, one hundred and sixteen industrial plants had already successfully implemented TPM. Sixty percent of them were Toyota group companies and their suppliers, demonstrating the close relationship between TPM and Just in Time production. The TPM aims to:

1. **Maximize equipment effectiveness:** involves the complete elimination of equipment failures and defects, eliminating losses and waste associated with equipment operation;
2. **Autonomous maintenance by operators:** involves operators in maintenance activities, although there is trade union resistance in some countries;
3. **Small group activities:** The company promotes workforce activities on a day to day basis.

Originated in the auto industry, TPM has expanded into semiconductors, food, pharmaceuticals, paper, printing, cement, ceramics, petrochemicals and oil refineries, among others.

## Company Global Performance

TPM consolidates failures and waste into a creative approach, using time as a common link. Thus, **Working Time** is defined as the total journey time that company works. In the case of a hospital or power plant, for example, it would be seven days a week, twenty-four hours a day.

From then on, we will be discounting the time spent on failures and waste, creating indexes that will selectively signal machine and equipment performance problems, operation failures and product defects.

**Total Productive Maintenance (TPM)**

| Working Time | | | | |
|---|---|---|---|---|
| Available Time | | | | Downtime |
| Operating Time | | | Breakdown | |
| Productive Time | | Speed Loss | | |
| Zero Defect Time | Rework | | | |

Source: Introduction to TPM. Seiichi Nakajima

We start with the Working Time and extract the Downtime, which is the time that machines or equipment failed, preventing production from occurring. The remaining time, i.e. when the machines and equipment are running, is called Available Time. See in the following diagram that the available time index (ati) equals the Available Time divided by Working Time.

**Available Time**

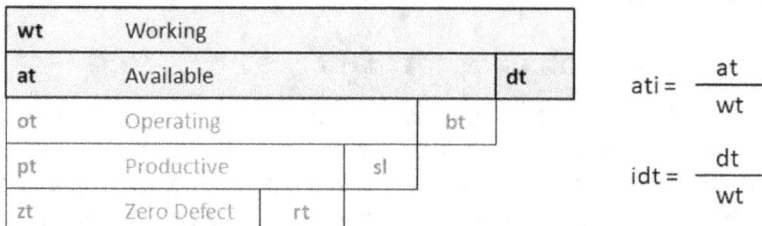

From Available Time is now subtracted the production Breakdown Time, which represents operational waste, staff shortages or operational failure. The remaining time is called Operating Time. The operating time index (oti) is obtained by dividing the Operating Time by the Available Time.

### Operating Time

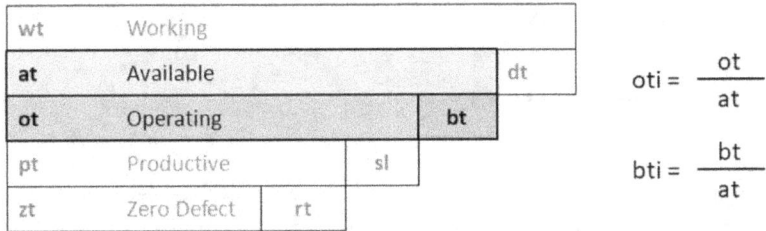

Operating Speed indicates how close the process has come to the theoretical production cycle. See that the effective cycle is calculated by dividing Productive Time by np, the number of products produced. Then, the theoretical cycle is divided by the effective cycle to obtain the Operating Speed index (osi).

### Operating Speed

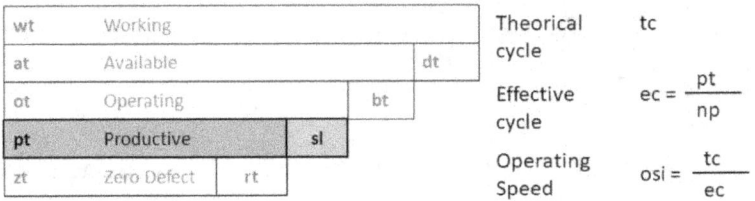

In calculating the Operational Performance Index (opi) below, the Productive Time Index is multiplied by the Operating Speed. In the numerator the Productive Time is replaced by the total quantity of products multiplied by the effective cycle. With this, we extract from Operating Time the loss of operational speed of production. The remaining time is called Productive Time.

**Operational Performance**

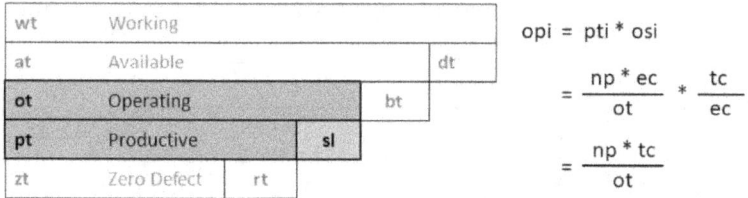

Considering the product quality, the Productive Time is deducted from the time spent reworking defective products, creating the Zero Defect Time (zti) index. At this time, the production system worked fully, with no downtimes, breakdowns, defects, or rework to fix them.

**Quality Products**

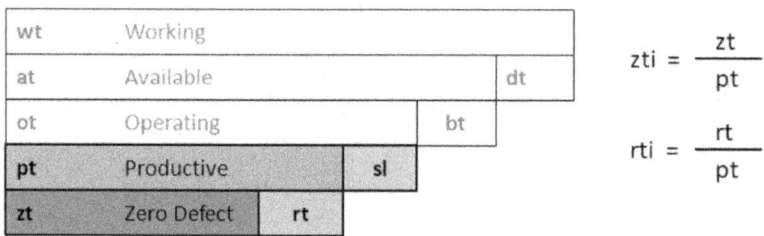

Finally, the company's Global Performance is achieved by multiplying the four indices of Available Time, Operating Time, Operating Performance and Zero Defect. Following is the equation that results in the Global Performance Index (gpi).

## GLOBAL PERFORMANCE

**gpi = ati * oti * opi * zti**

This indicator of the company's overall performance is very interesting since intermediate indices provide a selective and detailed analysis of the sources of problems. Masterfully, TPM has turned time into a decision support tool that brings together concepts as diverse as stopping machines, wasted labor, and faulty parts. Following is a summary of the TPM indices:

- **Available Time Index (ati)**: Equivalent to Available Time divided by Working Time, that is, the amount of time that machines and equipment do not fail and production can occur.
- **Operating Time Index (oti)**: Equals Operating Time divided by Available Time. Considers the portion of time without a breakdown in production, due to lack of personnel or failure in operation.
- **Operational Performance Index (opi)**: This is equivalent to the multiplication of Operating Speed by the Production Time Index, reflecting the production operational speed losses.
- **Zero Defect Index (zti)**: Equivalent to Zero Defect Time, which produced only perfect products, divided by Productive Time, i.e. represents the portion of time free from rework on defective products.
- **Global Performance Index (gpi)**: This is the multiplication of the four indices above, corresponding to the overall performance, considering the problems caused by eventual failures and waste to which the Process is subject.

For clarification of the formulas, follows the graphical representation of the production counters, including the total of products produced and those that were effectively dispatched.

**Production Counters**

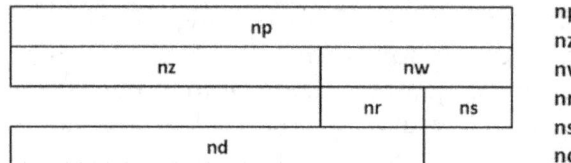

| | |
|---|---|
| np | produced |
| nz | zero defect |
| nw | reworked |
| nr | recovered |
| ns | scratch |
| nd | dispatched |

The Process produces **np** products, of which **nz** are free of defects, and **nw** does need rework. Of the latter, **nr** products are recovered and added to **nz**, resulting in **nd** dispatches. The **ns** unrepaired products are recycled as scratch.

## *Just in Time (JIT)*

The most interesting dispute between Westerners and Easterners in the second half of the twentieth century was not the race for the best total quality or productive maintenance program. Toyota's JIT made the difference by promoting a new measure, more important than reducing costs.

This does not mean that the improvement in quality has not made a difference. But while Deming has put the Orientals at least a decade ahead in the race for quality, Westerners have run after them and made up for the lost time. In this case, there was no disagreement on the merits of the matter, everyone agreed it was important to improve the quality.

But there was something else. Suppose in the 1970s, a salesman negotiating with different buyers, one from Toyota and one from GM. The seller asks each one:

- Would you like to increase your raw material order tenfold? In return, I give you a good discount.

What would each one answer? I bet the American would say yes and the Japanese would say no.

Which one would be right? What measures would each manager use? What would they rely on to decide? What are the principles behind each decision? Would that be a philosophical question? Would it be a matter of principles?

On the one hand, increasing Profit through cost savings was a well-known principle. Everyone knew, everyone agreed not to waste, and many cut costs in earnest. Why pay more for each piece? Wouldn't it be better to give in to the seller, increase the order and get a good discount on the raw material? As a result, the unit cost of the part would be lower and, if the sale price was maintained, there would be more profit. With idle capacity, it would even be able to maintain Profit and reduce the sale price, thus conquering more market.

At that time, cost reduction was Measure #1 at GM, because Cost Accounting dictated the company's management rules. As a result, the Cost Accounting system influenced GM to opt for cost savings.

## Measure #1 is Return on Investment

At Toyota that was not so, Measure #1, which guided managers' decisions, was **Return on Investment**. The Japanese buyer had no doubt, as the philosophical principles that created Just in

Time chose to optimize Investment, even if it meant spending more. This was the priority principle followed by the Japanese managers. At Toyota, cost savings were considered Measure #2. In fact, they accepted rising costs to protect investments, processes were designed that way. JIT production suppliers could make several customer delivery trips in one day. A cost-educated manager, on the other hand, would not agree with this and would try to concentrate everything on one delivery.

That was the real contest, accelerating the progress of the winning side. With JIT, managers' decision was most influenced by the principle that Return on Investment was more important. As a result, Cost savings were downgraded to Measure #2 in importance. This meant giving priority to reducing investments, even if it was necessary to increase costs.

In addition to Profit, the company's indicators gained one more equation and now looked like this:

**COMPANY INDICATORS**

$RI = NP / I$

$NP = (PS - RM) - (WF + OH)$

| | |
|---|---|
| RI | Return on Investment |
| I | Investment |
| NP | Net Profit |
| PS | Product Sales |
| RM | Raw Material |
| WF | Workforce |
| OH | Overhead |

Reviewing the equations, we see that increasing Net Profit is still desired, as it improves both measures. But note that reducing Investment only increases Return on Investment.

Following is the rise in industrial competitiveness of the second half of the twentieth century, which shows Western dominance systematically losing ground to Eastern industry in various areas of the market. Beginning in the 1970s, while Toyota's evolved Just in Time at full throttle, Western companies preferred to insist on Cost Accounting, seeking sophisticated correlations between fixed costs, products, and the process. Developed at Harvard University in the 1980s, the ABC management method unsuccessfully attempted to address accounting inaccuracies that attributed cost to products.

**Industrial Competitiveness**

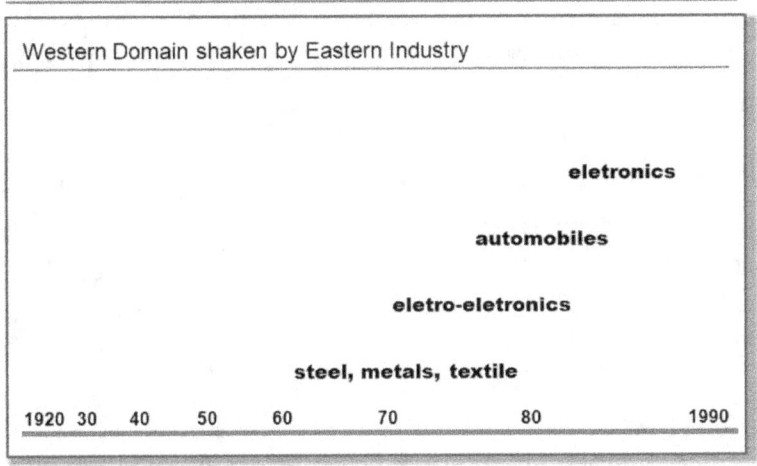

Source: The Race. Eli Goldratt e Jeff Fox. (adapted by author)

By the time Westerners realized that Return on Investment was a more important measure than Cost Reduction, Orientals had already gained considerable competitive advantage in the late 1980s. The consequence of this is that given the same situation, completely opposite decisions were made by managers on both sides of the world. Each investor and manager was unanimous in the belief that they were running their business better.

For those who still have questions about the seller's previous question and which buyer was right see the following chart for industry developments in the twentieth century. Since the 1970s, the product lifecycle has been dramatically reduced from several years to a few months, precisely due to the emergence of Just in Time production. Thus, under normal conditions, discounts would not justify unnecessary stockpiling, as there was a risk that competitors would launch new products that would run aground on our future sales.

**Industry Evolution in the 20th Century**

|  | 1920 40 50 | 60 | 70 | 80 | 1990 |
|---|---|---|---|---|---|
| Defects | 10% |  | <10% | <1% | ppm |
| Life cycle | decades |  | several years | few years | months |
| Machines | conventional |  | NC | automatic cell | automatic plant |
| Logistics | manual | MRP | JIT | MRP II | synchronized manufacturing |
| Inventory Turns |  | 2-5 |  | 5-20 | 30-80  >100 |

Source: The Race. Eli Goldratt e Jeff Fox. (adapted by author)

If we don't have sales, why would we need raw materials? As the life cycle of products fell, the eastern industry gained market, throwing news after news. Watches, once passed from father to son, began to be chosen to fit the clothes.

Other reflexes of the reduction in Investment are observed in the **Inventory Turns** indicators, i.e. the number of times the stock is renewed during the year. In nearly two decades, indicators have jumped from one to three digits.

The philosophies of western and eastern administration were so different in a certain period of history that the results could only be measured in practice in the presence of the chief arbiter: the world market. The rush for the most efficient management philosophy led Western companies to revise their plans and correct the route from the late twentieth century.

# 80's: The West Turn Over

From 1953 to 1992, despite two oil shocks that shook the world, Japan achieved the highest rates of economic growth among the industrialized countries. In 1989, Japanese companies shook the United States with the purchase of Rockefeller Center and Universal Studios. On December 7, 1991, Jamari França published in the Jornal do Brasil:

*"... Forty-six years after the fatal blow to the Japanese, the discussion in the United States focuses on one question. Have we won the war? The Japanese, armed with their millenary wisdom, turned a military defeat into an economic victory. Today, Japan has a trade surplus with the United States of $45 billion, and the debt-ridden US government could not pay its employees this month if it did not raise money in the market by selling bonds that have their main buyers in the Japanese.*

*By the end of the year, 35 US governors will have gone to Tokyo for investment. - They come here because they are not fools. Investments mean jobs. We need money, declared in October, to The Washington Post correspondent in Tokyo, New York Governor Mario Cuomo. Xenophobic Americans, such as Chrysler kaiser Lee Iacocca, denounce a Japanese attempt to dominate the United States by taking advantage of American free-trade ideology, imposing its automobiles, electronics and even threatening to control American culture through the acquisition of record labels, such as former CBS, current Sony and Universal (Matsushita) studios. ... "*

At this time, I was leading a project that connected three hundred microcomputers on a local network in a Ford Electronics Division factory in Brazil. This unit was rated Quality #1, the highest degree of quality conferred by the corporation. Around eighteen thousand car radios were manufactured daily, almost all of which were exported to the United States, Europe, and Japan. The factory floor had workstations distributed along with conveyor belts that carried parts of the radio in assembly, calibration, and functional tests.

The stations were automated, the operator removed the radio from the conveyor belt and coupled it to a base full of contacts that injected and measured signals. Controlled by a micro, the station powered an instrumentation bus connected to signal generators, multimeters, oscilloscopes and other instruments used in the calibration and testing of radios. Application software assisted the operator in automating procedures.

The project of interconnecting these stations was challenging for the time, as there were three hundred of them on the factory floor. Similar architectures were already used by Ford in other facilities around the world, except that the stations were connected to a PDP-11 Digital Mini-Computer. Through serial ports, three hundred cables ran out of a suspended-floor, air-cooled data center, circled the factory floor and reached the stations. At the Brazilian plant, there was no super mini, refrigerated room or 300 serial cables. In its place, local area network architecture, new at the time, running through a coaxial cable installed along the tracks.

The Data Collection and Analysis System consisted of hierarchically interconnected LANs totaling 380 standard IBM PC XT/AT micros. Instead of the minicomputer, dual IBM AT server structures, distributed across the shop floor, dynamically backed up data, traversing the workstations and collecting information for the plant's Statistical Process Control. There was fault-tolerance on dual servers through detection, reconfiguration and automatic recovery mechanisms in case of errors. It was an incredible experience working for a decade in this Ford Quality #1 project.

One day in the early 1990s, a factory engineer commented on the great repercussions caused by the book "The Goal", written by Eli Goldratt and Jeff Fox. The book was known to be a soap opera starring a factory manager trying to save everyone from the threat of closure. He proposed a new management philosophy that was giving excellent results wherever it went! After reading and rereading the book a few times, I was sure there was really something extraordinary going on. I needed to personally check the concepts that jumped between the lines of that soap opera, as it seemed that a new writer had appeared on the set.

I took a plane and went to the Goldratt Institute in New Haven, New York City, to attend a workshop conducted by Jeff Fox himself. The classes were small, the room had two rows of tables forming a V, with a dozen people seating face to face.

They were investors and business managers who had already read the book and were trying, like me, to learn more about the new philosophy. Jeff, at the top of the V, began by telling us that the previous class was made up of a group of US Army generals.

Seeking a reference, he counted the stars on their shoulders. There were a total of forty stars on the generals' shoulders and they wanted to know why the Japanese were buying New York.

Guided by an efficient Socratic method of teaching, Jeff was asking us questions and turning answers into conversations. Slowly and gradually, it led us to our own discoveries. In this way, it facilitated the transposition of the barriers erected by our education and avoided the contamination by the non-invented-here syndrome.

Due to the great interest that the theme aroused at the time, I left there willing to spread that knowledge in Brazil. Then, I spent some years teaching the Theory of Constraints through workshops in major Brazilian cities. I met Professor Goldratt personally in a lecture in Rio de Janeiro and I handed him the brochure of my workshop, asking for his autograph. He read it and asked me: - How big is your company? - Small, I answered. He signed the flyer, smiled and told me to go ahead. I was relieved that it was not precisely him the bottleneck of my business.

Beginning in 1984, the Theory of Constraints has been applied to companies such as Ford, HP, Bausch & Lomb, GE, GM, Xerox, the US Air Force, and many others seeking to outperform competitive global performance. In July 1992, Rudolph Hohn, president of IBM Brazil, gave an interview to Exame Magazine, saying that his bedside book was "The Goal" by Eliyahu Goldratt. "I want to understand how organizations in tomorrow's world will work," he said.

In 1993, IBM Brazil organized a training entitled "Executive 2000", dedicated to the sons of the executives of large companies who would inherit the business from their parents. The intention was to point them to the stone path, showing the state of the art of business administration. IBM made a general call, calling on consultants to present their ideas and I was honored to be one of the selected.

Using the same Socratic method by which I had learned, I presented to future entrepreneurs Eli Goldratt's Theory of Constraints at an event held at IBM Gávea, an executive study center, located in a heavenly place in the Tijuca Forest of Rio de Janeiro. Concepts of the old world of costs and the new world of gains were being presented. The future executives would decide their way forward.

## *Theory of Constraints (TOC)*

At the end of the twentieth century, the progress of the eastern industry exerted unprecedented pressure on western companies, forcing them to dramatically improve the services they provided to their customers. It was urgent to adopt a new philosophy with the potential to bring substantial improvements in company management in the age of coveted continuous improvement or kaizen. This would require the company to have an information system to guide the decision-making process of its managers.

However, cost-focused companies were often drowned in oceans of data, complaining about the lack of information. Then, the Theory of Constraints (TOC) was created by the physicist Eliyahu Goldratt. Like Deming, Goldratt has devoted much of his educative effort to alert the world of the bad influences of Cost Accounting. To make room for new management theories, the dogmas of the world of costs should first be eliminated. The key was to deconstruct outdated models by repeating ad nausea warnings against Cost Accounting. Other books, including The Race, Theory of Constraints, and The Haystack Syndrome, stand out in Goldratt's bibliography, citing distortions caused by the world of costs and suggesting the respective alternatives of the newly created world of gains.

At the time, there was a serious and justified concern, as everyone knew that simply copying the manufacturing techniques of Japanese products would not be enough to reach them. Deming mentioned this and Goldratt used to draw a rising exponential curve, representing the performance of the Japanese industry and its respective growth. Then, he draws an exact copy of the curve, shifting it a little to the right. The copy would be the industry that tried to reproduce its biggest competitor, but with some delay, since it would take some time to study and implement the copy. The following figure, which reproduces this situation, shows the distance to the competitor increasing over time, even as the company captures and copies the competitor's techniques regularly and accurately.

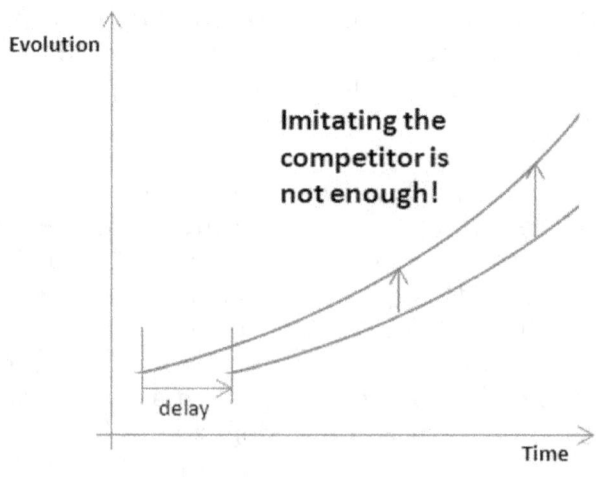

At the time, this meant the obligation of the western industry not only to match but to outpace the growth of Japanese competitors. Reaching them seemed like a very difficult, almost impossible challenge.

## Measure #1 is the Gain

Goldratt, however, used the Net Profit formula to convince everyone that managing the cost world was very information-dependent. All terms of the equation are costs except Product Sales, he insisted. The amount of entries associated with costs represents a lot of information. How many expense outlets are there in the business? Which expense to cut, if almost everything is important? Even supposing it possible to overstate all costs, the total could at most go down to zero. That is, the reduction strategy is limited by the simple fact that costs are finite. From a certain point, it is becoming difficult to keep reducing costs.

To change the paradigm, Goldratt took the Net Profit equation and obsessively focused on analyzing the term of **Product Sales**. This is the only term that contributes positively to Net Profit, he raged. He also stated that, unlike costs, sales volume has no limits, i.e. the sky is the limit. In addition, Product Sales has less accounting information to handle. Goldratt mentioned the following indicators:

**FINANCIAL INDICATORS**:

From the world of costs:

- **Return on Investment (RI)**: Equals Net Profit divided by Investment.
- **Net Profit (NP)**: Product Sales Revenue minus Raw Material, Labor, and Overhead Costs.
- **Cash Flow (CF)**: If the company has cash, Cash

Flow does not matter so much. If the company has no cash, nothing else matters.

From the world of gains:

- **Gain (G)**: This is the rate at which the system generates money through sales and equals revenue from Product Sales minus Raw Material expenses. The term "Throughput (T)" was used by Goldratt for this indicator.
- **Inventory (I)**: It is all the money the system invests by buying things that the system intends to sell.
- **Operating Expense (OE)**: This is all the money the system spends turning Inventory into Gain. It is the sum of the Workforce and the Overhead.

The following equations reflect the bridge between the world of costs and the world of gains:

**COMPANY INDICATORS**

$$RI = NP / I$$

$$NP = (PS - RM) - (WF + OH)$$

$$G = PS - RM$$

$$OE = WF + OH$$

$$NP = G - OE$$

$$RI = (G - OE) / I$$

The table below shows different scales of importance of the measures that differentiated companies that lived in the world of costs and those that migrated to the world of gains. In management dominated by Cost Accounting, the Operating Expense is Measure #1. The Gain comes in second and Investment in third and last position.

| **IMPORTANCE SCALE OF MEASURES** | | |
|---|---|---|
| Order | World of Costs | World of Gains |
| #1 | OE | G |
| #2 | G | I |
| #3 | I | OE |

In the management philosophy proposed by Goldratt, the novelty is the Gain as Measure #1. This made the difference and led western companies to overcome the exponential growth of the eastern concurrency. Since the Japanese had already taught about the importance of Investment, Goldratt considered Investment as Measure #2. Lastly, the company's fixed costs, represented by Operating Expense that definitely dropped from the top of measures podium.

What does this order mean? We saw that in Just in Time production, the reduction in investments justified the increase in costs. This same commitment also applies to the world of gains. Another commitment, unprecedented and unique in the world of gains, is to protect the Gain, even if it requires investing more or having higher expenses.

## Constraint determines performance

Since Gain is the most important measure, how to increase it? How can we at least guarantee that it will not decrease? To start thinking, it is crucial to note that Gain only happens when there is a sale. What can facilitate or prevent a sale from occurring? Consider the Deming process definition, rewritten below:

*"The process is divided into steps; the work enters in one step, changes its state and continues, having as a client the next step. At each stage there is production, that is, something happens, causing different output, until the final stage, intended for the consumer."*

Therefore, for a sale to happen, the product must go through all the stages of the process. Goldratt realized that the world of gains would deal with a **chain of actions**. The performance of this chain would be determined by the strength of its weakest link.

From that, came the definition of **Constraint**, which is anything that limits a system from achieving higher performance relative to its goal. How many are the weak links in a chain? For example, consider a fictitious factory where there are no faults or waste, i.e. machines do not stop, the operation is not interrupted, and products have zero manufacturing defects.

**What is the production volume of this factory?**

Working Time = 5 days x 8 hours x 60 min = 2400 min

As shown in the figure above, the production consists of four steps. Step A spends 4 minutes on initial product processing and transfers it to step B which only lasts 2 minutes. Then, step C takes 12 minutes processing the material before moving it to D, the last process step that takes 6 minutes to get the product ready to ship.

Assuming the factory's Working Time is 2,400 minutes per week, how many products would be manufactured during this time? Think about it before you look at the answer below.

To determine factory capacity, simply calculate how long it takes a product to manufacture. It would be correct to add the time spent on each operation and conclude that the production processes for 4 minutes in step A, plus 2 in B and so on, resulting in 24 minutes of processing in all four steps?

This reasoning does not determine the capacity of the factory since the production line is a chain of actions, functioning simultaneously. When commissioned, the factory is able to dispatch a product every 12 minutes because this is the exact time that step C lasts. Capacity is determined by the speed of the slowest step, i.e. one product every 12 minutes. In this way, the 2,400 minutes Working Time would produce two hundred products per week.

The constraint or bottleneck of the factory is therefore said to be the step C. What happens when you invest in improving another step than the bottleneck? There would be more return on investment in buying a new machine to reduce step D in two minutes? No, not at all. Net Profit would be the same as the factory's production would still be two hundred pieces a week.

But what if we use this same investment to reduce the time from step C from twelve to say ten minutes?

In that case, the 2,400 minutes would produce two hundred forty products or twenty percent more. Suppose the investment in step C proceeded so that its time would fall by half, that is, to 5 minutes. What would be the production of the factory? See the updated diagram below:

**The constraint has passed to D!**

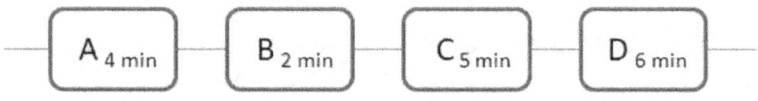

Working Time = 5 days x 8 hours x 60 min = 2400 min

Note in the new diagram that the 5 minutes of step C no longer restrict factory production as much as step D, which takes six minutes processing the product. As a result of the investment that made stage C faster, the factory started producing 400 pieces per week, twice as many as before. The improvement in step C evolved the bottleneck, making step D the new process constraint.

Now it would make sense to consider the investment mentioned at the beginning of a new machine for D. The world of gains philosophy accurately clarifies the return on investment opportunities and warns of critical points in the process that need special care.

## Decision Process

What is the procedure that ensures that we are always trying to explore the most of our bottleneck? In addition to evolving and accelerating bottlenecks that constrain the business, it is critical to address the existing constraint.

The critical stage of the process should never lose speed. If the speed of step C was halved at the original factory, which produced two hundred products per week, the processing time would increase from 12 to 24 minutes. With that, the two thousand and four hundred minutes of the factory's Working Time would produce one hundred products or half as well.

Care must be taken to ensure that the bottleneck is ALWAYS protected so as not to be delayed or wasted. As Goldratt insistently reminded, a second that gets lost in the bottleneck can never be recovered, it's a loss forever.

The following decision-making process ensures continuous improvement for those who use the theory of constraints.

**TOC DECISION PROCESS:**

1. Identify the system constraint(s);
2. Decide how to exploit system constraint(s);
3. Bribe everything else to the previous decision;
4. Evolve the system constraint(s);
5. If, in the previous steps, a constraint has been broken, return to step 1, without letting inertia cause a system constraint.

The third step is perhaps the most important in companies' daily lives, especially after a few rounds of bottleneck improvements. There will always be a restriction in any chain of actions. We must know how to live with it and, under no circumstances, allow the bottleneck of the process to be delayed.

## P&Q Factory

To demonstrate how the Theory of Constraint can help managers with their decision-making logic, there is a factory that is immune to distractions that often blame themselves for poor corporate results. The P&Q Factory, an exercise conducted at the Goldratt Institute workshops and published in its book "The Haystack Syndrome", gives no room for apology. The fictional factory portfolio has only two products: P and Q. Using TPM in the P&Q Factory description, it can be stated that:

- **ati = 1** Factory equipment runs nonstop for the entire working time, the available time index is 1.
- **oti = 1** There is no break in the operation, because the employees of the factory are perfect, i.e. the operating time index is also 1.
- **opi = 1** At the P&Q factory there is no speed loss in production, machine tool change time is zero. This all represents an operational performance index of 1, like the others.
- **zti = 1** There is not even any rework on defective products as P and Q are manufactured without defect, i.e. zero defect index is 1.

Thus, as shown in the table below, the gpi, or global performance index, calculated by multiplying the four indexes mentioned, is equal to 1 as well.

| Index | Initials | Value |
|---|---|---|
| Global Performance | gpi = ati * oti * opi * zti | 1 |
| Available Time | ati | 1 |
| Operating Time | oti | 1 |
| Operational Performance | opi | 1 |
| Zero Defect | zti | 1 |

Using the week as a unit, the factory's working time is 2,400 minutes per week. Due to unitary gpi, this time is all used in the process to manufacture P and Q at the highest quality and speed possible.

There is no difficulty to move the P&Q Factory products because the market has the potential to buy up to 100 pieces of P and 50 pieces of Q per week. Just produce and dispatch the products, and the market guarantees the purchase within these limits. The unit sales price is preset at $90 for P and $100 for Q. If production exceeds market limits, products become stranded.

As for fixed costs, there are no surprises. P&Q Factory Operating Expense is $6,000 per week, encompassing all Labor and Overhead expenses. This does not include the cost of the raw material, proportional to production.

The engineering of the P&Q Factory presents the manufacturing process in the following diagram, showing the production flows that result in P and Q. The raw materials used in the process are P-Part, RM1, RM2, and RM3, at costs respectively of $5, $20, $20 and $20. The P&Q Factory process consists of four steps: A, B, C, and D, meaning there are four jobs with different skills in the process.

As shown in the diagram, RM1 raw material enters Step A, takes 15 minutes processing, then goes to Step C for 10 minutes and ends in Step D, which assembles product P.

Another flow starts with RM2 being processed in Step B for 15 minutes, continuing to Step C for a further 5 minutes and reaching P and Q assembly steps D. Note that the central flow is used in both P and Q fabrication, that is, to manufacture one of each, it is necessary to process RM2 twice through B and C.

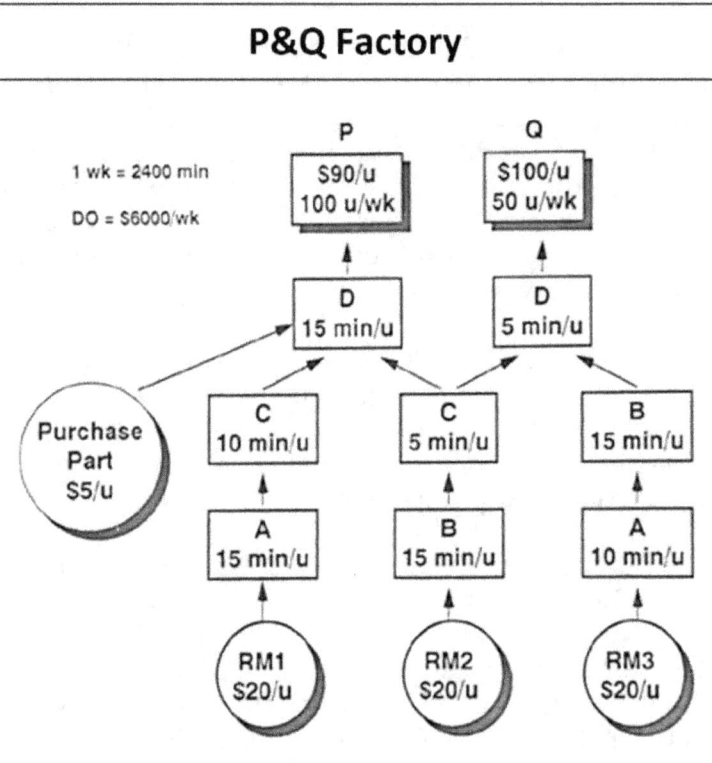

**P&Q Factory**

1 wk = 2400 min
DO = $6000/wk

Lastly, RM3 spends 10 minutes in Step A, then is processed for 15 minutes in Step B and goes to Q mounting at Step D. P&Q mounting Steps D are processed in respectively 15 and 5 minutes.

## How much profit does the P&Q Factory?

What is the maximum net profit that P&Q Factory can earn per week? Think about the time each stage has for producing P and Q. It is known that the workload of the Steps is two thousand four hundred minutes a week. The answer follows in the next paragraphs.

The first impulse would be to do a simple calculation, adding the gains made with each product and decreasing the operating expense. To calculate the unitary Gain of P, subtract from the Selling Price ($90) the cost of Raw Material P-Part ($5), RM1/RM2 ($20 each), resulting in $45. Multiplying it by 100 pieces results in $4,500 total Gain for P. The procedure for Q is similar, as follows:

NP = G(P) + G(Q) - OE
G(P) = ($90 - $5 - $20 - $20) * 100 = $45 * 100 = $4,500
G(Q) = ($100 - $20 - $20) * 50 = $60 * 50 = $3,000
NP = $4,500 + $3,000 - $6,000 = $1,500

Add in P and Q Gains and decrease $6,000 from Operating Expense. The Net Profit result is then $1,500, right? Wrong!

According to the TOC decision process, the first step is to identify the constraints of the system. From the production forecast for a given mix of P and Q products, the loads placed in each Step are calculated and compared to the existing availability of 2,400 minutes per week. The table below shows a production forecast of 100 x P and 50 x Q:

**PRODUCTION FORECAST** (minutes): 100 x P + 50 x Q

| Step | P x100 | Q x50 | Total |
|---|---|---|---|
| A | 15 x 100 = 1500 | 10 x 50 = 500 | 2000 |
| B | 15 x 100 = 1500 | 30 x 50 = 1500 | 3000 |
| C | 15 x 100 = 1500 | 5 x 50 = 250 | 1750 |
| D | 15 x 100 = 1500 | 5 x 50 = 250 | 1750 |

P is known to use 15 minutes from Step A, multiplying by 100 pieces results in 1,500 minutes. Product Q requires 10 minutes from Step A, which times 50 totals 500 minutes. As a result, the mix will require 2,000 minutes of Step A, which is less than the availability of 2,400 minutes per week.

Redoing the accounts for Step B, product P puts a charge of 15 minutes, i.e. 1,500 minutes for 100 pieces. The charge generated by product Q is 30 minutes in two separate 15-minute jobs. Multiplying by 50 pieces, you have another 1,500 minutes. This results in the sum of 3,000 minutes, which exceeds the availability of Step B of 2,400 minutes, which characterizes and identifies a constraint.

Redoing the calculations for Steps C and D, both are charged 1,750 minutes per week, i.e. subject to existing availability. A constraint has been identified and the P&Q Factory is unable to meet market demand. As a result, we reach step 2 of the decision process and must decide how to exploit the constraint, i.e. Step B. What is the best production mix? How many P&Q products to offer to the market? What is the most profitable product?

Goldratt drew attention to the criteria used in the world of costs that would, in principle, make product Q more profitable:

- The unit selling price of P is $90. In case, Q is $100, a bit higher;
- P unitary raw material cost is $45. In case, Q is $40, a bit lower;
- The unit gain of P is $45, while that of Q is $60, thirty percent higher;
- Adding the unit load of Steps A/B/C/D results in 60 minutes for P and 50 minutes for Q.

By these criteria, a cost manager would not have much doubt in producing Qs to the fullest. This would allocate 1,500 minutes from Step B to produce 50 pieces of Q, leaving a total of 900 minutes for P production. Since Step B processes 15 minutes per piece, P production would be 60 pieces per week.

The suggestion from the world of costs would be to change the factory production mix to 60 x P and 50 x Q. See the result in the following table and note that Step B is busy throughout the full 2400-minute working time.

**PRODUCTION FORECAST** (minutes): 60 x P + 50 x Q

| Step | P x60 | Q x50 | Total |
|---|---|---|---|
| A | 15 x 60 = 900 | 10 x 50 = 500 | 1400 |
| B | 15 x 60 = 900 | 30 x 50 = 1500 | 2400 |
| C | 15 x 60 = 900 | 5 x 50 = 250 | 1150 |
| D | 15 x 60 = 900 | 5 x 50 = 250 | 1150 |

The factory's net profit would then be calculated, after the decision to favor product Q, with a mix of 60 x P and 50 x Q:

NP = G(P) + G(Q) - OE
G(P) = $45 * 60 = $2,700
G(Q) = $60 * 50 = $3,000
NP = $2,700 + $3,000 - $6,000 = - $300

Operated this way, the factory would show red numbers, losing $300 a week. But note that the decision to privilege Q took into account the "product profitability", a distortion created by the world of costs. It's just a mirage, disguised as the great global. In fact, there is only the company profit.

In the world of gains, one has to exploit the constraint to the maximum, that is, to make the most money by working the bottleneck. Offering Q to the market, the factory earns $60 and invests 30 minutes from Step B, meaning it gets $2/minute with the bottleneck working. With product P, the factory earns $45 and invests 15 minutes from Step B, thus receiving $3/minute for the bottleneck work.

Which one is best? The suggestion from the world of gains is to privilege product P. This would allocate 1,500 minutes from Step B to produce 100 pieces of P, resting a total of 900 minutes to make Qs.

Considering Step B processing 30 minutes per piece, the production of Q would be 30 pieces. The suggestion is to change the factory production mix to 100 x P and 30 x Q. Redoing the production forecast from the world of gains:

**PRODUCTION FORECAST** (minutes): 100 x P + 30 x Q

| Step | P x100 | Q x30 | Total |
|---|---|---|---|
| A | 15 x 100 = 1500 | 10 x 30 = 300 | 1800 |
| B | 15 x 100 = 1500 | 30 x 30 = 900 | 2400 |
| C | 15 x 100 = 1500 | 5 x 30 = 150 | 1650 |
| D | 15 x 100 = 1500 | 5 x 30 = 150 | 1650 |

The factory's Net Profit is then calculated, after deciding to privilege product P, with the mix of 100 x P and 30 x Q:

NP = G(P) + G(Q) - OE
G (P) = $45 * 100 = $4,500
G(Q) = $60 * 30 = $1,800
NP = $4,500 + $1,800 - $6,000 = + $300

Now the factory earns $300 positive Net Profit per week. Much better! The TOC decision-making process was able to reverse the bad results that were being obtained at the P&Q Factory and brought the much desired blue color to the financial indicators.

What if the factory was real? What if there are machine shutdowns, breakdowns, speed drops, defects, and rework? In this case, gpi will be less than 1, and the ati, oti, opi, and zti indices will point to the likely causes. Widespread problems such as strikes or power outages can affect virtually every step of the process. Localized problems, such as defective components, would affect one Step only. It is the responsibility of each Step to inform its operating conditions, for example by means of charts recording their respective TPM indices.

What if the market was real? The bottleneck may be in the market! In the exercise with guaranteed sales, the bottleneck was within the company. It was an internal problem, identified and restricted to Step B of the P&Q Factory Process. Another completely different scenario may occur when there is an offer of more competitive products, either due to higher quality or lower prices. If production becomes difficult to sell, the Process should change to improve price and/or quality or business needs to be fully rethought. Focusing on a niche of customers, providing them a new and enchanting experience, is a widely used solution today. If it works, the return of satisfied customers increases sales and consequently the volume of production. Again, the bottleneck returns to the company, and the cycle of improvement continues.

JOSÉ MOTTA LOPES

# 10's: Life goes on

In 2017, a century after the invention of the Henry Ford factory, there are no more Japanese buying New York. China is the Asian power of the time. Attesting to the western recovery that began in the 1980s, US President Barack Obama stated in his farewell speech:

*"If I told you eight years ago that America would reverse a major recession, recover the auto industry and trigger the longest job creation in our history... you would say we were wanting too much, but that's what we did. That's what you did. You are the change."*

Coincidental or not, that same day the US Secret Service issued an intelligence report warning of the risk of world conflict.

*"Problems in the economy will widen the gulf within society and out of this emptiness will emerge populist leaders promising to restore order and jobs. Populism will grow on the right and the left, and some leaders will use nationalism as a form of domination. Gigantic migratory flows will result in a loss of social welfare and increased competition for jobs, which in turn will lead to more nationalism, more populism."*

Lack of international cooperation would have disastrous consequences, especially now that climate change is increasingly present, requiring consensus from all.

## *The goal is the great global*

To make the great global a reality, we definitely

need working organizations more than ever, and working well. Organizations are made up of people and governed by philosophies that determine their behavior. To guide decisions toward the global optimum, a complete and comprehensive Information System model is needed, consisting of simple combined elements that express the best management and administration practices.

This Information System would be based on the following assumptions:

- Companies are organizations formed by investors who hire managers to assist in the task of management;
- Investors are solely responsible for the conception and design of the Information System;
- The development and operation of the Information System is the responsibility of investors and managers;
- The Information System should enable investors and managers at each level of the company to always have, at any time, a global view of the organization and its role in globalization.

But that is not the case today. Obviously, we need to better manage conflicts between the company's departments, between companies, within the governments' machines, between companies and governments, between labor and capital, between right and left, between rich and poor, between countries, between borders and citizens. A huge volume of capital circulates around the world, gained and lost a lot, not for lack of consultants.

CEOs are given astronomical numbers to steer companies down paths that lead to success. Similarly, aviation commanders are responsible for taking off planes with hundreds of passengers on board and cross oceans amid storms. Except for rare exceptions, all flights land safely. Compare it now to a CEO who tries to keep the company's competitiveness high by resisting market turmoil and avoiding forced landings for hundreds of employees. Why is there no autopilot for businesses like we have them for airplanes? Economic turmoil seems to be less predictable phenomena today and more difficult to control than gusts and storms over the oceans.

Is economics giving up on being a more exact science? What are the real factors to consider when looking for the global optimum? What is the direction of true globalization?

## *The sum of the local optima almost always takes us away from the global optimum*

The information system with the right measures should guide investors and managers, at any time, towards the global optimum. Not only pointing in the right direction but also helping to keep a steady course. Only the great global frees future generations from the brink of the dark abyss of competition and conflict.

To focus on the global optimum, one must avoid the local optima that misrepresent or interfere with the perception of the global vision. At the slightest oversight, traps satisfying illogical combinations of local optima create mirages of the global great. One must have wisdom and persistence in the pursuit of the true direction of globalization. The mantra to repeat many times is: The sum of the local optima almost always takes us away from the global optimum. Keeping this in mind is already half the problem solved.

## The Conflict in the Pyramid

An individual with certain skill and resources creates a small business. Applying his knowledge, he elaborates a process that transforms market-acquired raw materials into products he intends to sell. In the beginning, he is the do-everything. Buy, produce, sell, invoice, pay and receive. Market acceptance is good and sales grow rapidly, driven by word of mouth from satisfied customers.

The diagram below represents this stage of business, where the investor is very close to everything and everyone. It captures information directly from the process and makes virtually instant decisions, streamlining business operations. Free of distortions in information and decisions, the business goes on and on.

**Investor creates Process**

As sales increase, it needs to work harder and harder. It optimizes the process and multiplies to a certain extent. There comes a point where he realizes that he needs to change the way he works. From that moment on, the skilled investor will no longer act as before, as it becomes vital to increase control over the process.

## *Pyramid Expands Control*

The investor alters the process and has distributed the buying, producing, selling, invoicing and receiving tasks among business managers. In pyramid form, a multilevel structure establishes a hierarchy of managers. Here's a typical diagram:

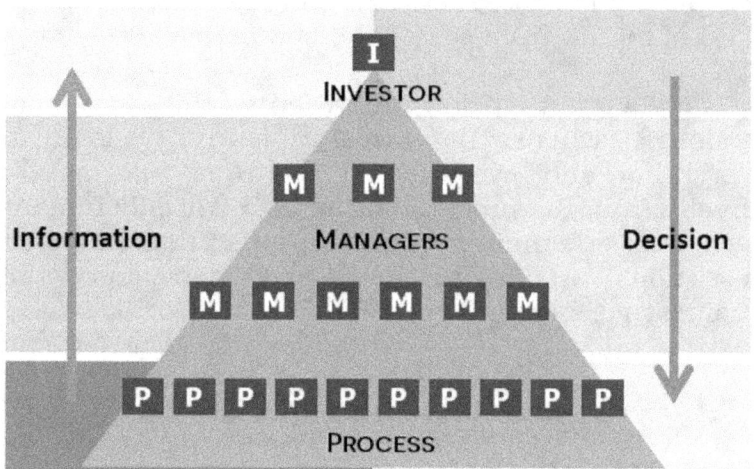

As the business grows, it needs to add levels to the pyramid. Depending on the activities performed, this occurs when the human limit is reached, which usually sets a maximum of fifteen subordinates per person.

This structure has been widely employed by various types of organization throughout history. From armies to religions, the hierarchical pyramid is unanimous when it comes to management. The expansion of the commanding power of investors and managers requires that they relate to the immediately upper and lower levels.

The main duties of managers are:

- Receive and relay investor orders to command the process;
- Capture process information to keep the investor updated.

The investor's plan is for each manager to have command power over the entire pyramid of subordinates below him. The investor also needs managers to be responsible for capturing and reporting the accurate status of the process.

## *Manager cycle*

Obviously the company must continue to deal with the flow of information and decisions that circulate between the process and the investor. If this flow is interrupted, or even impaired, the company suffers serious risks. Therefore it is paramount that each pyramid manager is able to handle the two pairs of inputs and outputs listed below:

| Name | | Description |
|------|--|-------------|
| **Din** | Decision Entry | Order received from boss |
| **Dout** | Decision Out | Order relayed to subordinates |
| **Iin** | Information Entry | Information Received from subordinates |
| **Iout** | Information Out | Information transmitted to boss |

From training and proper investor commands at the top of the pyramid, managers must fulfill their role by guiding their subordinates in conducting the process. Similarly, managers should capture process information, analyze it and inform the investor of relevant facts. Note that each manager has only access to the immediate adjacent levels in the pyramid structure, that is, their boss and their subordinates.

The diagram below shows in detail the flows of information, analysis and decision to which each manager of the pyramid is individually submitted:

## Information-Analysis-Decision

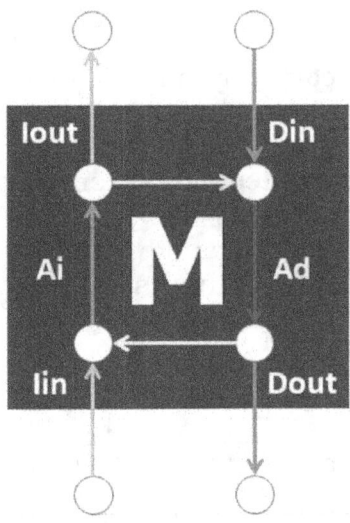

| Name | | Description |
|------|--|-------------|
| Ai | Information Analysis | Manager evaluates process operation |
| Ad | Decision Analysis | Manager interprets company command decision |

- The up arrows represent the path taken by the information. The subordinates cause the information originated in the process to be propagated through the pyramid until it reaches the input Iin. It is the manager's responsibility to perform the Ai analysis of the information received before passing it on to his immediate boss through the Iout exit. Accordingly, the information is expected to follow its path towards the investor, located at the top of the pyramid.

- The down arrows express the Investor's command to be propagated through the pyramid structure until it reaches the process. Thus, decisions made at the upper echelons of the company are expected to result in immediate management orders received at Din. The manager must perform the Ad analysis and generate a set of Dout decisions for his subordinates, following company directives.

- The horizontal arrows reflect audits performed by good managers. By reporting Iout information to the immediate boss, the manager may anticipate a future investor Din decision. Likewise, after a Dout decision that affects the process has been triggered, a future reflection on the Iin entry that consolidates the change is expected.

## *Pyramid Distorts Information/Decisions*

Undoubtedly, the hierarchical pyramid solves the investor's problem of increasing control over the process. But at what cost? See in the example below that a three-level pyramid requires information and decisions to pass through three managers to reach the investor and the process respectively.

## Distortion in Information and Decision

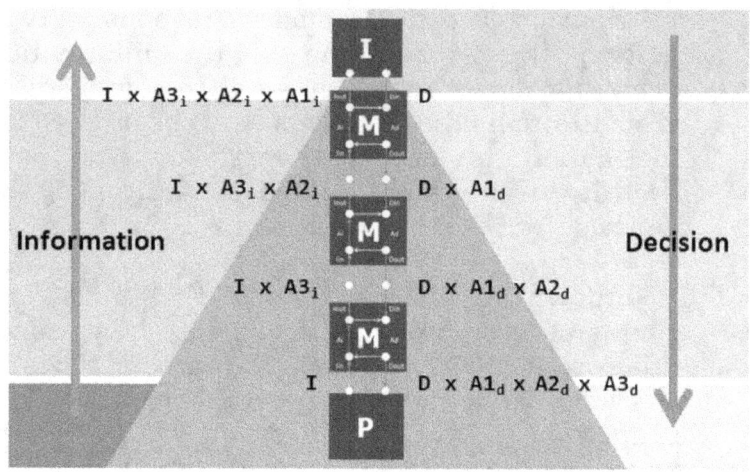

Consider the investor passing on to his first echelon a decision D that should be directed to the process. At the same time, an information I is captured at the lowest level of the pyramid near the process. In the small startup where the investor does everything, there is no distortion in decision and information, contact is straightforward.

In the hierarchical manager structure, only level 1 manager receive the "pure" decision D from the investor. He will then analyze and relay the D1out decision to the second level, taking into account the interpretation of how the D decision should be implemented by their subordinates. See below the equation as it looks:

**D1out = D1in * A1d = D * A1d = D2in**

Repeating the reasoning for a hierarchical structure of managers with n levels, the decision that will arrive at the process can be calculated as follows:

D-Process = D-Investor * A1d * A2d * A3d ... * And

Similarly, "pure" information is captured by the third-tier manager. It performs A3i information analysis and transmits the resulting information to its boss's I2in input at level 2:

I3out = I3in * A3i = I * A3i = I2in

Considering all analysis propagated by the managers of each level, the information will reach the top of a n-level pyramid with the following interference:

I-Investor = I-Process * A1i * A2i * A3i ... * Ani

Then, there are interferences in decisions and information, represented by A1d, A2d ... And, A1i, A2i ... Ani, respectively the decision and information analysis that have been applied by managers, at their respective pyramid levels. Distortions in information and decisions are proportional to the number of levels in the hierarchical pyramid. The higher the pyramid, the greater the likelihood of information and decisions will be distorted.

## *The conflict in the pyramid*

Apparently there is a conflict in the hierarchical structure of managers:

- The pyramid expands control over command and information between the investor and the process. To enlarge, one must add levels to the pyramid;
- The pyramid distorts information and decisions that circulate between the investor and the process. To avoid, reduce the levels of the pyramid.

The following diagram shows the details of the conflict in the hierarchical manager pyramid. For the investor to be successful with the process, it is necessary to increase control as well as to avoid distortions in information and decisions. Both are fundamental requirements for the intended success.

## Conflict Diagram

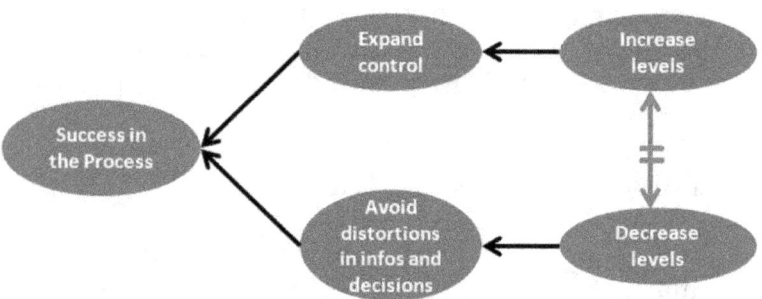

## Conflict Analysis

By analyzing the diagram components individually we can evaluate their strength:

- Increasing control has as prerequisite increasing levels in the manager hierarchy. There is no reason to doubt it.
- To avoid distortions of information and decisions, you should limit the height of the pyramid, i.e. have fewer levels.
- One prerequisite is the opposite of the other, as indicated by the unequal arrow in the diagram.

How to solve this dilemma? Would it be better to favor one side? Or displease them both and stand on the fence? Another option would be to go for a magical solution that pleases both sides and evaporates the conflict. Is it possible to identify the weak point of the conflict by looking carefully at each ellipsis and arrow on the diagram? First, we assure how strong the conflicting components are. For example, increased investor control and the absence of misstatements in manager information and decisions are vital to a company's success. Neither of these two requirements can be waived.

Another strong arrow is that of conflict itself, as you cannot raise and lower levels at the same time. That leaves two arrows to analyze:

- increase levels to extend control
- lower levels to avoid distortion

Which is the weak point of the conflict? To answer that, ask yourself:

- Can you extend control without increasing pyramid levels? Difficult, given the human limitation.
- How to avoid distortions in information and decisions without lowering the levels of the pyramid? What if there was a measure that would guide managers?

The solution to the conflict in the hierarchical pyramid is to find the right measure to help investors and managers to avoid distortions in their decisions and in the analysis of process information.

## *Measures evolution*

Every 30 years, since the 20's, there have been major changes that guide corporate investors and managers. See in the table below that the ranking of the measures presents differences during the evolution occurred in the western and eastern countries. Since the mid-twentieth century, due to fierce competition, the right management philosophy has determined success for the winning side.

| Years | 20' | 50' | 50' | 80' | 10' |
|---|---|---|---|---|---|
| Philosophies | global | western | eastern | western | global |
| Cost Reduction | #1 | #1 | #2 | #3 | #3 |
| Return on Investment | #2 | #2 | #1 | #2 | #2 |
| Gain Increase | - | - | - | #1 | #1 |
| Kaizen | - | - | Yes | Yes | Yes |
| Ampli Business | - | - | - | - | Yes |

Looking at the company's Net Profit formula, it can be seen that virtually all of its terms are costs, except for Product Sales. Costs also represent most of the company's accounting entries. Cost Accounting has met challenges in two world wars, occupying the #1 rank since the 20's. Cost savings was the most influential measure to investors and managers around the world aiming to increase Net Profit. However, the fundamentals of Cost Accounting have been shaken over time. Terms like "product profit margin" were losing their meaning.

The quality revolution, started by Deming in Japan in the 50's, was reinforced by the Kaizen, a concept of Japanese culture that other languages need a couple of words to express: continuous improvement. In the 70's, while Toyota was evolving Just in Time at full speed, Western companies still preferred to insist on Cost Accounting, seeking sophisticated correlations between fixed costs, products, and the process. The Japanese opted for Return on Investment more important than Cost reduction, highlighting the difference between eastern and western decision-support philosophies. The result was the Japanese buying New York in the 80's.

"Tell me how you measure me, and I'll tell you how I will behave. If you measure me in an illogical way, do not complain about illogical behavior". This phrase, by Israeli physicist Eli Goldratt, creator of the Theory of Constraints, stressed the importance of choosing the right measure to guide investors and managers. He turned the game on Westerners after promoting Gain to Measure #1. He used the Net Profit formula to convince everyone that managing the cost world was very information-dependent. All terms are costs, he exaggerated. What expense to cut if everything is important? We are drowning in a sea of data, complaining about the lack of information! With the world of gains, Goldratt changed the paradigm, obsessively focusing on the analysis of product sales. It's the only term that contributes positively to the Net Profit equation, he said. Unlike cost savings, Gain has no limits. That is, the sky is the limit.

## *Ampli Business*

From now on, to guide investors and managers in their decisions toward the great global, an Information System model consisting of simple, combined elements that express best management practices is needed. The Ampli Business philosophy proposes a four-tiered standardization effort:

1. Company Indicators
2. Cyclo: The Gain Machine
3. bAmpli: The Business Amplifier
4. bAmpli Circuits

Just looking at the bAmpli Circuit with 4 Cyclos below, it is known that:

- The investor is the "+" at the top left of the circuit;
- The investment is a bAmpli Business Circuit, formed by Cyclos numbered 1 through 4;
- bAmpli from Cyclo 1 invests on Cyclos 2 and 3;
- bAmplis from Cyclos 2 and 3 share their Profit;
- And reinvest it in the Cyclo 4.

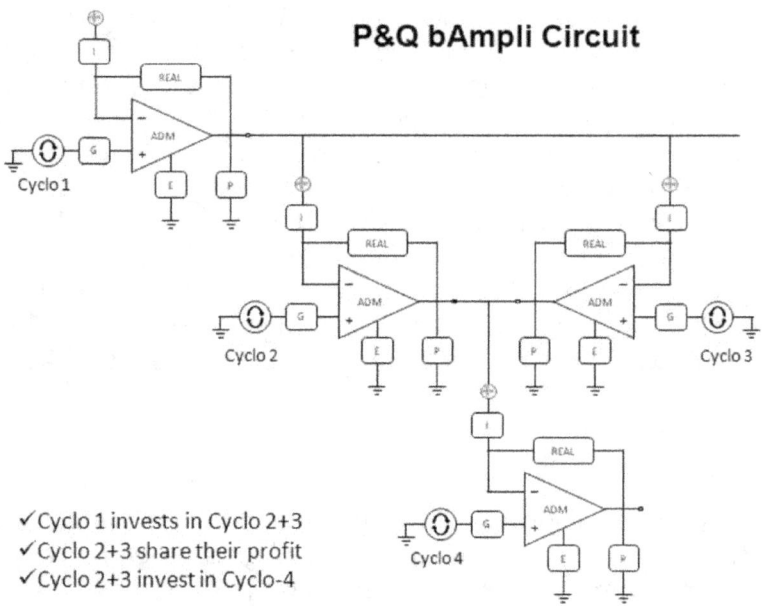

This 4-Cyclo bAmpli Circuit expects to make a profit to be returned to its investor, i.e. the "+" at the top left of the circuit. The next chapters will introduce the Ampli Business components and show more details about this P&Q bAmpli Circuit.

# Process Cycle

The Information System model has so far brought together valuable allies, incorporating concepts originating from SPC, JIT, TPM, and TOC into one of the most powerful combinations of decision support tools ever assembled in history. However, to assist investors and managers in decision-making toward the global optimum, relationships between Process Steps, suppliers and consumers need to be further deepened. How to provide first-class support for long-term trusts, as required by rule six of Deming's process specification? This is what I can do for you; here's what you can do for me.

Let's add a new tenth rule to Deming's Process:

**10. The Process is a closed loop that consumes products of nature and transforms them into other products of nature.**

In fact, this new rule is nothing new. Raw materials are eventually purchased and entered into a Process that generates products for sale. Joining the ends of the Process with the Earth, everything comes out of Earth, everything comes back to Earth. Products are bought, treated, combined and become other products to be sold. If the goal is globalization, at least the vision of the globe has emerged! In the world of gains, the sky is the limit, and the priority is to increase the gain. How to guarantee the gain today and always? Theory teaches that the constraint determines the performance of the process. It also teaches that we must take good care of it because time lost in the bottleneck is an irrecoverable loss! What is still lacking to guide investors and managers to decide towards the global optimum?

The operation of the Process Steps does not have a linear, one-time, and done behavior. The processing sequence of Steps repeats endlessly with each new product! Assets are always entered in a Step, are processed for some time and go to the next Step. This is repeated simultaneously in all Process Steps all the time. It looks like Process acts as n-stroke engine or n-pole generator, where n is the number of Process Steps. Each Step individually contributes with its speed and energy to keep the Process Cycle spinning. Everyone needs to keep up the pace, the teamwork can't stop. The time taken by the slowest step is what determines the performance of the process cycle, in this case, the spin speed. Spin? What turns? See in the following diagram that products and money cycle in opposite directions.

**PROCESS CYCLE**

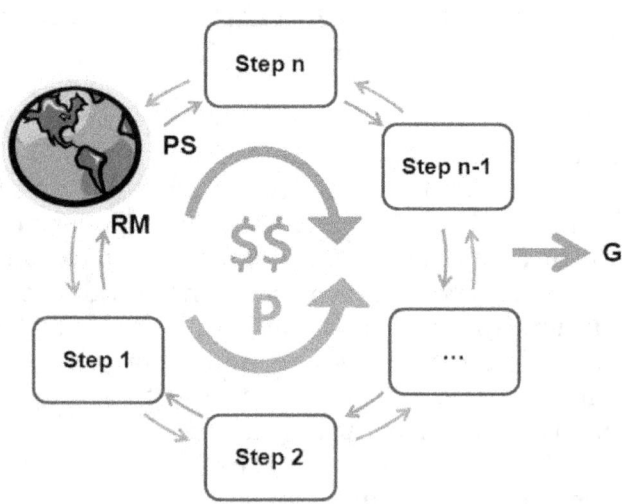

At the top, Earth's first arrow to "Step n" indicates the money from the consumer market that pays for Product Sales (PS). This money is used to pay Raw

Materials (RM) used in the Process Steps. The remaining balance is the Gain (G), which contributes to the profit of the company that invests in the process.

On the other hand, the outer arrows leaving Earth to "Step 1" represent the assets that traverse the path in the opposite direction. Raw materials are purchased from the market, entered into the Process and become products that the company intends to sell.

The steps depend on each other to keep both streams spinning simultaneously:

- Assets collected in the market being transformed into products sold;

- Money from selling products to the market by remunerating suppliers.

These two streams are closely related, one only happens together with the other. Without payments there are no raw materials in production, without raw materials there are no revenues.

How to explain the forces that make the Process Cycle spin? Returning to the chain of events mechanism, used in the definition of the constraint, it appears that first there is a need for a demand for the product in a given market. If this happens, just design the Process. From there, the consumer shows why it is the main link of the production line, as rule nine of the Deming Process says. With the "vital energy" released by product demand, the market consumers spin the Process Cycle. The spin speed is determined by the Process constraint.

To fit into the Process Cycle, the Steps need not necessarily be tied to the same warehouse, company or country. A sales channel, for example, has distributors and resellers in addition to the factory. The end user buys from the dealer who buys from the distributor, who in turn buys from the factory. They are all part of a process where products circulate in the channel from the factory to the end user. Authorized partners capture sales in the market, receive compensation for trade and service of products, and send money back to the factory.

## *P&Q Overseas*

The P&Q Factory from the previous exercise decided to expand its business to a distant country. To this end, it founded and installed in this country the company P&Q Overseas, in order to promote P&Q products.

The logistics of the new company found that transportation between the factory and the new market takes twelve hours by plane or thirty days by sea. Container shipping would make the business viable. The price of air travel is far more expensive and would undermine the competitiveness of P&Q in the new market.

The P&Q Overseas Process Cycle begins with logistics that removes a batch of products from the P&Q Factory and transports it to the country. Then, as shown in the following diagram, the shipment goes through customs and meets import procedures, a task that lasts a week, both by sea and air. As soon as they are cleared through customs, the products are entered into P&Q Distribution's warehouse.

## P&Q Overseas

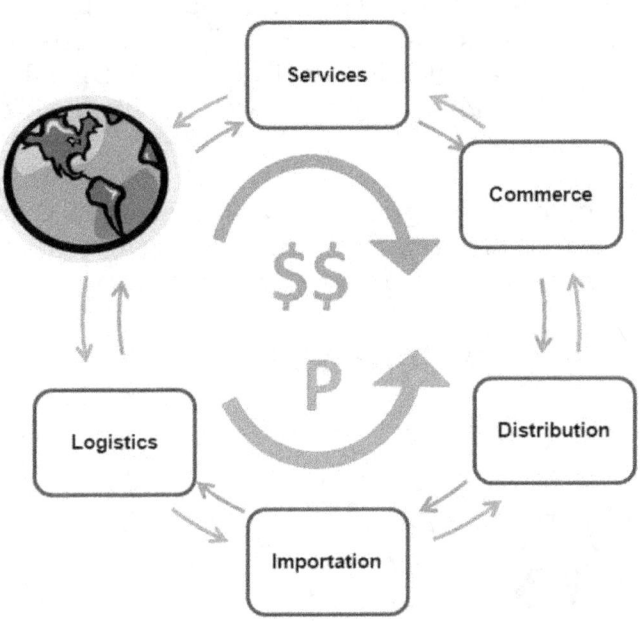

In order to increase channel capillarity, the distributor will not act directly with end users. The customers will be distribution channel partners, including sub-distributors, stores, VARs, OEMs and service providers. As a result, the P&Q Overseas Process Cycle will reach the end user only through authorized Commerce and Service partners, as pictured above by their respective Process Steps.

How to describe the operation of this authorized P&Q trade and service network using their respective Process Cycles? How these cycles are connected?

## P&Q Distribution

In principle, air transport is considered to be a high cost. Using containers on the sea route, shipments take five weeks from factory pick-up to the end of customs clearance. Because customers can't stand waiting all this time, P&Q Distribution will invest in enough inventory for five weeks of sales.

The following diagram shows the Process Cycle to be used in P&Q Distribution, where all authorized agents' purchase orders circulate in the country.

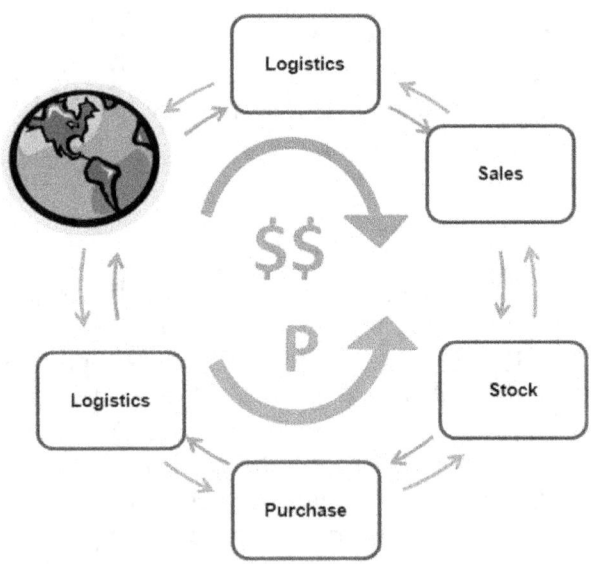

**P&Q Distribution**

The Purchase Stage periodically generates orders from the P&Q Factory for stock replenishment. In the absence of a crystal ball, past sales analysis gives a clue to market behavior over the next five weeks.

Depending on current inventory and sales forecast, we order from the factory the minimum order needed to protect sales. The Process Cycle continues with incoming shipments entering Stock. Acting independently of Purchase, the Sales Step processes orders, removes products from Stock, and ships them through logistics to authorized partners.

What can be done to accelerate this cycle through which all the P&Q products circulate in the country? It is not part of P&Q Overseas business to invest in points of sale or services inside the country. Therefore, the success of the P&Q channel will depend on authorized partners. The company intends to create partnerships across the country by nominating sub-distributors, stores, VARs, OEMs and service providers to cooperate in the P&Q product channel.

Authorized partners are paid a good sales commission and in return provide basic product support. Marketing actions encouraged by the factory promote the exposure of P&Q products in the country. The P&Q channel training introduces the Commerce and Service Process Cycles for partners interested in leveraging their respective businesses. This strategy practices in the country the philosophy of "This is what I can do for you; here's what you can do for me".

## P&Q Commerce

As seen in the following P&Q Commerce Process Cycle, each merchant is encouraged to invest in their own inventory to expedite prompt delivery to users and service providers in their region.

## P&Q Commerce

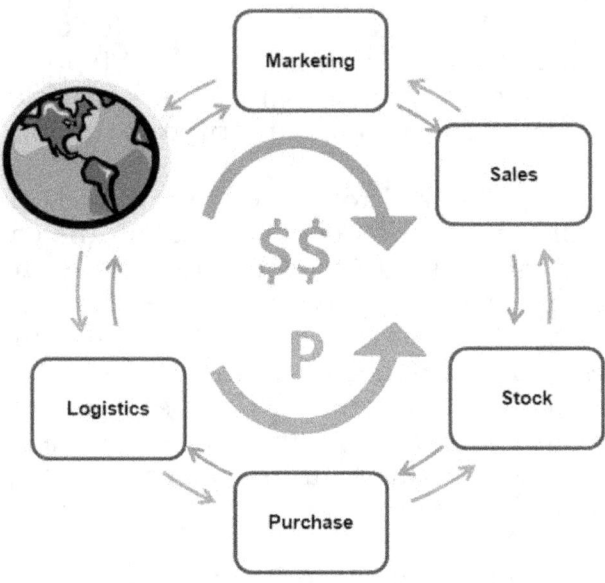

The Commerce Agents Process Cycle rotates products through buying and selling orders and ends in Marketing, which brings end users closer to authorized P&Q agents. The online store created by P&Q Distribution can be customized for each authorized partner, displaying product technical specifications and a shopping cart application that accepts orders over the Internet. Thus, users have the facility to select the point of sale or service center closest to their work or residence.

## P&Q Services

In addition to business partners, there are partners who specialize in project, installation, configuration and maintenance services related to P&Q products. Technical assistance does not need stock as the channel encourages professionals to purchase products from nearby authorized dealers. Unlike P&Q Commerce that manage product orders, note that the P&Q Services Process Cycle circulates service orders.

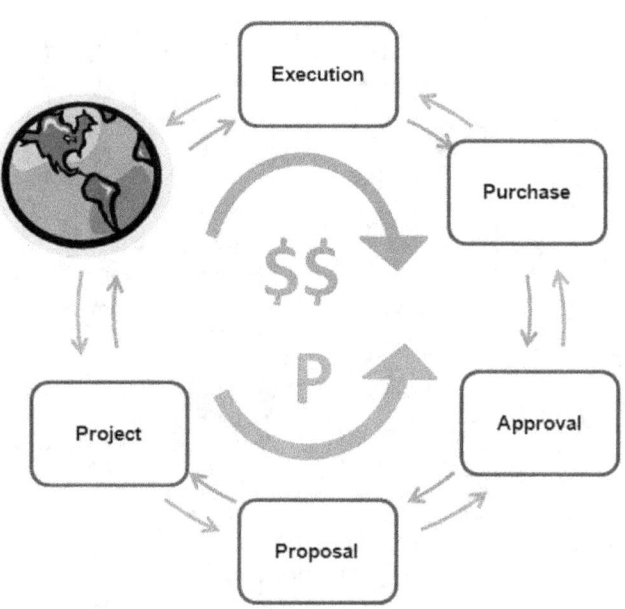

The cycle begins after the customer requests a service. In response, the customer is sent an initial project with the solution offered, accompanied by a price proposal, deadline, and other supply conditions. The next step is to get Proposal Approval. Hence, the cycle proceeds with any Purchases that may be required and the Execution of the Order. The service does not even have to include dispatching of P&Q products, for example, in case of maintenance or simple installation and configuration.

## Interconnected Cycles

What is the relationship between the P&Q Overseas Process Cycle and the Process Cycles of authorized Commerce and Services partners? The diagram below shows the three cycles.

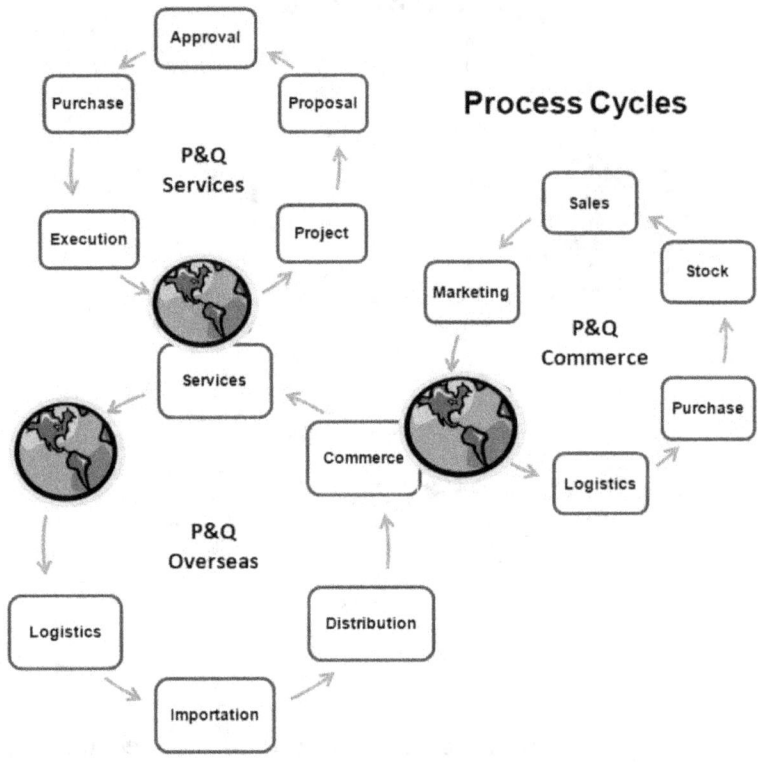

Together, one gear moves the other, the three cycles act as a single machine. Each round of the Process Cycle of an authorized P&Q Commerce also accelerates the P&Q Overseas Production Cycle as it demands stock replenishment through purchase orders to the distributor. The cycles of authorized P&Q Services strengthen the installed base in the new market, leaving customers and partners very satisfied.

The launch of the P&Q Channel in the country includes a website with technical specifications of the products, as well as an online web store. The P&Q Channel begins operations by moving a hundred SKUs (Stock Keeping Unit) between the factory and the country, including products, accessories, parts, etc.

As seaborne shipments arrive from the factory every five weeks, within a few months P&Q Distribution's stock problems begin to emerge. On one side, there is too much stock of some items. In contrast, unexpected sales cleared other inventory items. What are the consequences of this?

Having too much stock is bad because it hurts Measure #2 which tells us to cut back on investment to increase return on investment. One way out would be to promote excess items. Having fewer inventories is worse, as it hurts Measure #1 that protects the Gain from lost sales! Stock holes can freeze sales of certain items for some time. Worse than losing sales is losing a customer, especially because of a lost sale. Gain is lost now, as well in the future.

To fill the holes in P&Q Distribution's stock you need to replenish the stock faster. Could an air route be used in case of stock holes? Think how you would decide.

The cost would be higher, of course, but in return, the stock would be replenished in a week. In the world of gains, a higher expense to protect sales is justified. As a result, P&Q Distribution has installed a low-level inventory control alarm and an air shipment may eventually be triggered by the Purchase Step, replenishing the low inventory SKUs.

## *Project Guide*

After the stock holes were filled and minimum inventory levels were adjusted, P&Q Channel sales continued to grow. Now, the air shipment always arrives before any item clears.

P&Q Commerce partners report that they are excited about their Process Cycles spinning faster. Gain is happening more often in the same amount of time and with that, their Profit has increased!

However, even because of the success of the trade, partners from P&Q Services complain that they are unable to handle all requests. Although they have already reinforced staff, they argue that project and other service specialists are still lacking. The most important thing to consider is that customers like P&Q Services' innovation, precisely because it offers specialists who help solve their problems. It will be difficult to change this, because at the first contact, the expert helps identify the best solution for the user and prepares a project. The commercial complements a proposal, sends it to the user and accompanies its approval.

Managers argue that specialists waste a lot of time with some customers who call repeatedly for minor changes or end up giving up authorizing services, even after all the project preparation and commercial proposal work. In addition, design changes always entail a general overhaul of the business proposal, i.e. more waste of labor. Channel P&Q investors and managers then face a conflict. On the one hand, the high salary limits the hiring of more specialists. On the other hand, there are clients who drop out of care even before the specialist is free. P&Q Overseas management has already noted certain stagnation in the speed of the P&Q Distribution Process Cycle through which all products traded in the country pass. How to accelerate the P&Q Services Process Cycle? Only then will the P&Q Overseas Cycle accelerate as well. The steps listed below from P&Q Services Process Cycle require optimization:

## P&Q SERVICES PROCESS CYCLE

- s1.user: go to the website, looking for a solution
- s1.user: choose products through website
- s1.user: choose authorized to hire services
- s1.user: contact authorized service

- s2.specialist: meets and identifies user solution
- s2.specialist: create project for user

- s3.commercial: quote project
- s3.commercial: send project / proposal to user
- s3.comercial: confirm user approval of project

- s4.operation: triggers any purchase orders
- s4.operation: run services

- s5.user: approves services and receives invoice
- s5.user: pays invoice for authorized assistance

First, user looks for a solution. After consulting product specifications on the website, user makes the purchase and finds an authorized dealer to request services. Starting second step, the expert attends authorized service, identifies the user solution, and creates a custom project. In the third step, the commercial staff prepares and submits the commercial proposal and accompanies its approval by the user. The fourth step is for operation personnel who perform the services. The fifth and last step returns to the user who approves the job and pays the invoice.

The problem happens in Step Three when, instead of approving the project and starting the operation, the user returns to the expert proposing a change to the project. With this, the Process returns to the second Step. But there is nothing wrong with the customer wanting to modify their purchase!

The way to solve the conflict was the creation of the Project Guide, an online virtual assistant that assists the user in preparing his project and its corresponding proposal. There is not so much variety for most of the popular solutions and automation should relieve the experts, freeing them up for more rational service.

The website shopping cart is adapted so that the Project Guide can provide online business proposals, including services. Through the Project Guide, the user can send notes/instructions to the expert and vice versa, i.e., the exchange of information for questions and eventual changes in the project is encouraged. The Guide also has educational material for users, professionals, and experts who want to deepen their knowledge.

The modified Process Cycle starts the same, with the user accessing the P&Q website. But this time, Step One has the new Project Guide as an assistant. The user feeds the Project Guide with customized information and is able to review his choices and make changes at will. If in doubt, he communicates by leaving a message, explicit instructions or questions to the experts. The Step only ends when the user clicks the project approval. Following you can see the complete Project Guide Process Cycle:

## PROJECT GUIDE PROCESS CYCLE

- s1.user: consult website and browse the Project Guide
- s1.user: feeds Project Guide with custom data
- s1.user: choose authorized for services
- s1.user: review project and proposal online
- s1.user: approves the project

- s2.specialist: reviews user technical design

- s3.commercial: reviews user business project

- s4.operation: triggers any purchase orders
- s4.operation: run services

- s5.user: approves services and receives invoice
- s5.user: pay invoice to authorized

The second Step starts with the specialist, only this time there are no customers waiting anxiously for service. It just responds to pending projects and releases approved projects. The commercial can interact too and makes the final review before the operation takes over. The remainder of the Process Cycle is unchanged.

In addition to eliminating bottlenecks, this exercise shows how to make the Process Cycle more stable by eliminating special causes that take the Process out of statistical control and waste resources. Note that now Steps two and three, where the expert and the commercial act, have become more predictable and professionals can prioritize the projects they will work on.

The practical effect of the Project Guide, highlighted by the arrow in the diagram below, shows the direct link established between authorized P&Q Trade and P&Q Services. This strengthened connection, which meets rules five and eight of the Deming Process, accelerates the P&Q Distribution Cycle, which appears in the lower right corner.

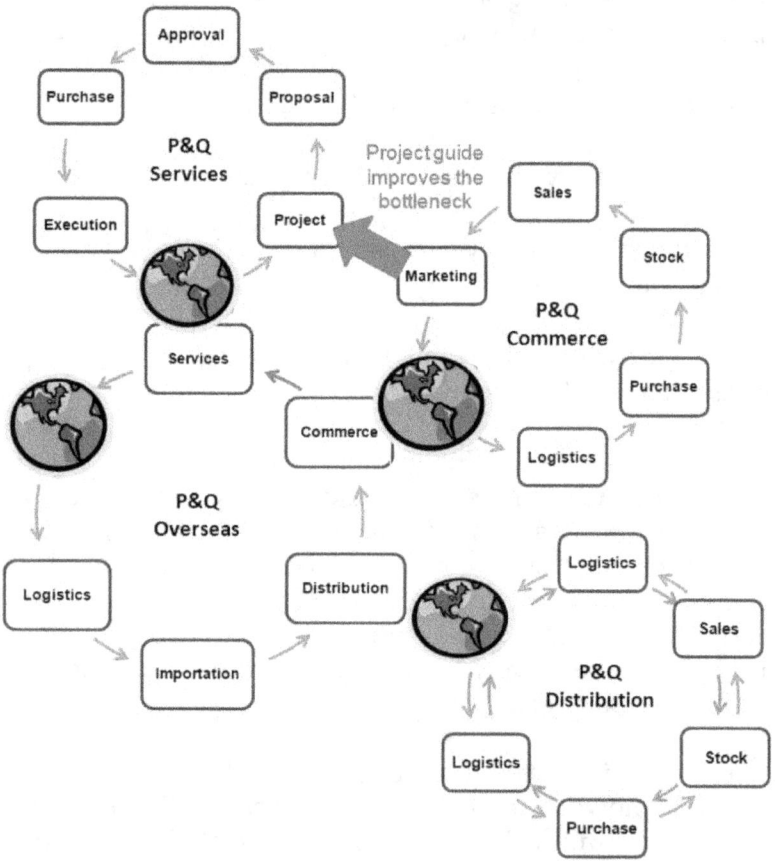

It is interesting to note that ALL channel business in the country is exposed on the same diagram. The process cycles of P&Q Commerce and P&Q Services represent not only the operation of a company but the entire set of trading and service partners in the country.

## Niche markets

Investors and authorized network managers have adopted a tool that sees out of the box of their companies. Without interference from local optima, they have the opportunity to focus on the global optimum.

As a result, the specialist is no longer a bottleneck in authorized technical assistance and is now part of a nationwide distributed P&Q Channel pool. Design Guide users now have an agile and engaging experience with expert support and freedom for last-minute changes. All of this, thanks to the Process Cycles that give managers and investors a global view of companies and their role in the great global.

After restrictions were fixed on the P&Q channel, the plant is once again the focus of attention, as Step B continues to be the bottleneck for the P&Q Factory. The following condensed diagram, called the **Process Cycle Diagram**, includes all P&Q business, starting with the factory:

- P&Q Factory Process Cycle that employs P-Part and RM1 / 2/3 raw materials to generate P&Q FOB products.

The remaining companies that cooperate in the P&Q Channel are also represented:

- From P&Q FOB products, P&Q Overseas imports and forwards the products to sales channel. It also authorizes and educates service providers.

- To do so, it has P&Q Distribution that transports the product from the factory, imports it according to the country's rules and transforms it into the local P&Q channel product.

Process Cycle Diagram

| | | | | | | | | |
|---|---|---|---|---|---|---|---|---|
| Services | User | Project | Proposal | Approval | Purchase | Execution | | Service |
| Commerce | Channel | Logistics | Purchase | Stock | Sales | Marketing | | User |
| Distribution | FOB | Logistics | Purchase | Stock | Sales | Logistics | | Channel |
| Overseas | FOB | Logistics | Importation | Distribution | Commerce | Services | | Service |

$RM → ← $PS
RM ← ← Product

Factory: P-Part, RM1, RM2, RM3 → A, B, C, D → P FOB, Q FOB

- In turn, P&Q Commerce partners purchase the nationalized products from the distributor, add a sales commission and sell them to P&Q users.

Although the products are the same, the FOB, Channel, User, and Service nomenclature reflects the transformations within the P&Q Channel in the respective Process Cycles. The authorized trading and service partners thus ensure the capillarity of the P&Q market in the country.

Interestingly, as much as there are cycles in the diagram, there is only the bottleneck B Step to be explored and raised. There is not much doubt about the decisions to be made to continue improvement toward the global optimum. Even those who do not take a direct part in the bottleneck know to what extent their performance can compromise the whole set. Everyone has the exact awareness that getting worse, anyone can become the bottleneck.

How to expand the experience of P&Q Channel investors and managers who have made decisions based on Process Cycles? The Niche Market diagram below shows that it all starts with the business model being accepted by a network of partners. Hence the Process is conceived and the market does the rest.

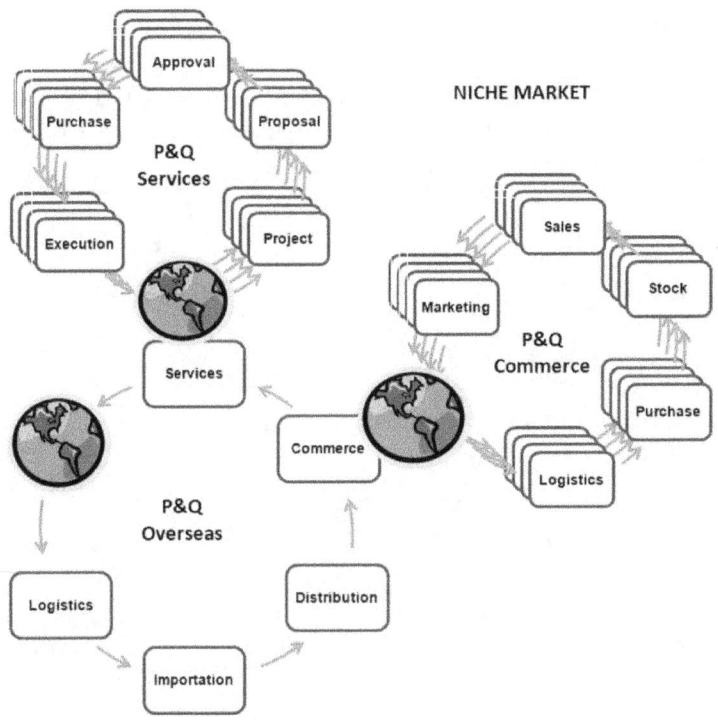

In practice, would anyone else be interested in participating? How to extend reasoning to everyone? Does this path lead to the overall great or is it just another local optimum in disguise?

Pursuing the philosophy of "This is what I can do

for you; here's what you can do for me", Process Cycles can go beyond the limit of private processes. As P&Q channel partners have done, Process Cycles can specify public standards that would establish close relationships of trust.

In this way, a customer could, for example, consult a niche market formed by a group of companies whose Process Cycle met certain specifications. In turn, suppliers would invest in adhering to globally recognized Process Cycles patterns.

By assuming a self-identity, Process Cycles can be used to link all business and drive continuous improvement to the market.

# Times of Gain

How to measure the process cycle? What measures to use? The Process Cycle measurement must consider that there are cash and product flows running through the cycle.

Flows occur at their own distinct times, as money from sales and raw materials can either be paid in advance, on delivery, or within a certain time frame. In contrast, assets always enter each Step, process for some time and advance to the next Step until they reach the consumer, already in the form of a final product.

In common, they travel the same cycle, but in opposite directions. Because it is a cyclical phenomenon, the Process Cycle has a period, as defined below.

- **Period (T)**: This is the time interval for a cyclic phenomenon to repeat itself. In the case of Steps, it is the time spent processing each product and can be measured in seconds, minutes, days, weeks, etc. For example, P&Q Factory Step B processes each unit for 15 minutes.

## *Normal distribution*

In the ideal factory exercise, Step B spends 15 minutes processing the RM2 raw material. It turns out that the period of the Step is not a deterministic variable. The period is indefinite, that is, it varies in practice because the processing times are not exactly the same, product by product.

If we make a control chart of the time taken by a

Step to process its assets, we will have variations due to common and special causes, i.e. its period originates from random, unpredictable events.

Subsequent measurements of the processing time of a Step generate a sequence of periods T(i) where "i" represents each product. **If the Process is under statistical control,** i.e. free of special causes, the distribution of T(i) values of the time that each Step lasts can be represented by a **normal curve**, one of the most appropriate probability distributions for modeling natural phenomena.

Expressed through the mean and standard deviation, the normal curve is bell-shaped, as shown in the figure below.

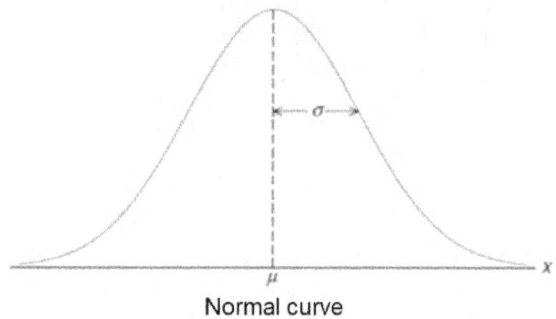

Normal curve

The **mean** indicates the central position of the distribution, and the **standard deviation** refers to the dispersion of the distribution.

If the distribution is accurate around the mean, we have an elongated curve. Otherwise, the curve flattens and the measurements spread, as can be seen in the two following curves, with the same mean and different standard deviations.

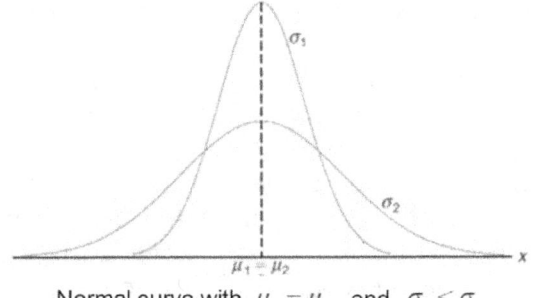

Normal curve with $\mu_1 = \mu_2$ and $\sigma_1 < \sigma_2$

The mean can be used to represent the period of the Step, and the standard deviation determines the confidence intervals. For example, there is a 99.7% probability that the measurement will be within the range (± 3 standard deviations) centered on the average, as shown in the following figure.

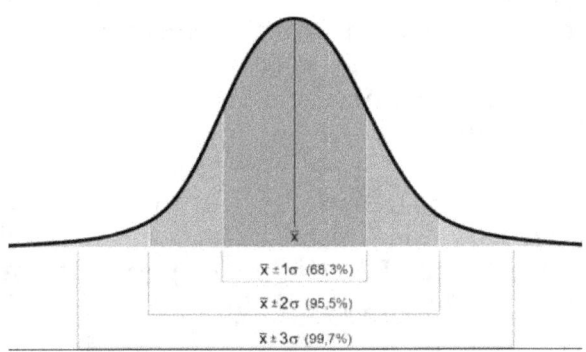

Therefore, if a Step spent processing its assets the sequence of periods T(i) for each product i = 1, 2, ... m, we have the definitions:

- **Mean Period (Tm)**: T(i) i = 1, 2, ... m.

- **Standard Deviation (Sd)**: T(i) i = 1, 2, ... m.

The Information System considers that the Process is designed to be stable, i.e. predictable over the processing period of each Step. With this, the Process ensures that the processing periods of the Steps are under statistical control, within the control limits established by existing common causes.

Any special causes must be isolated and treated, keeping smooth processing of the steps and consequently maintaining the process under control. Keeping predictable Gain timing is a prerequisite for continuous improvement toward the global optimum.

## *Process Spin*

The Process Cycle measurement can also be expressed by the inverse of the period, i.e. the frequency:

- **Frequency (F)**: The number of times a phenomenon occurs within a certain unit of time. In the case of the Process Cycle, it refers to occurrences during the Working Time, according to TPM definition.

Frequency can also be interpreted as spin, angular velocity, i.e. a number of complete cycles per unit of time. From Tm, the mean period of the Step, then calculate "w" as the Spin of the Step, through the equation:

$$w = \frac{\text{Working Time}}{\text{Tm}}$$

What is Spin for? It is known that the Process is divided into Steps. If the Step is precisely the Process bottleneck, then the Step spin is actually the Process Spin. In other words, if the bottleneck determines performance, Process Spin is nothing more than bottleneck Spin.

What is the Spin of the P&Q Factory from the previous exercise? The corresponding Process Cycle follows, showing the bottleneck in Step B.

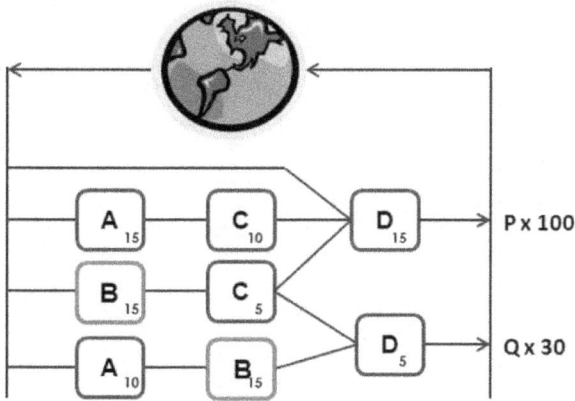

P&Q Factory Process Cycle

Dividing the Working Time by the fifteen minutes spent processing Step B, the bottleneck is triggered one hundred and sixty times a week.

## P&Q Factory Spin

$$w = \frac{\text{Working Time}}{\text{Tm(Step B)}}$$

$$w = \frac{2{,}400 \text{ min/week}}{15 \text{ min}}$$

**$w = 160$ /week**

This is the total number of uses from Step B during the Working Time. Double checking the bottleneck load for the product mix, in order to produce 100 pieces of P, Step B is used once per product. This leaves sixty uses of Step B. This allows thirty Q's to be produced, which use twice the bottleneck each. Bingo!

# Cyclo: Gain Machine

The diagram below shows Cyclo, a Gain Machine based on the Process Cycle. The Gain results from the difference in the money received from Selling Products and paid for the Raw Materials. Consequently, Gain results from the multiplication of speed by money, both to receive and to pay.

**Cyclo: Gain Machine**

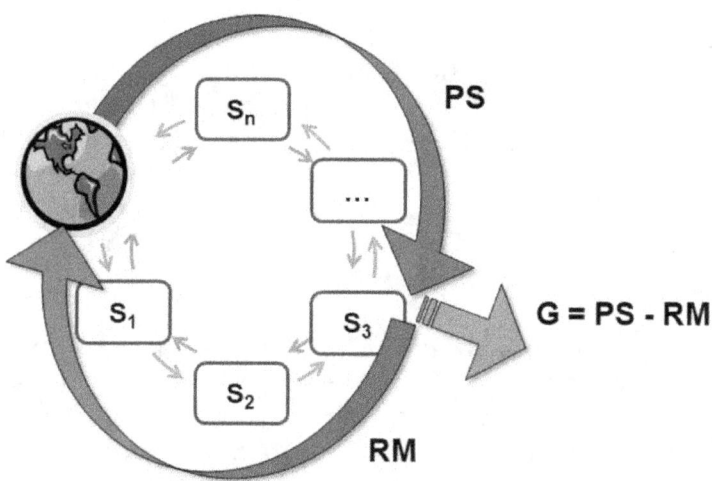

Nothing prevents this flow from assuming negative intermediate values, but a positive Gain value is expected to be sufficient to cover the company's Operating Expense and generate Net Profit.

- **Cyclo:** Gain Machine based on Process Cycle;

- **Gain G** ($/t): Flow resulting from the receipt of Product Sales and payment of Raw Materials;

- **Spin w** (#/t): Cyclo's spin speed is equal to the inverse of the period of bottleneck Step.

Gain (G), measured in money per unit of time ($/t) can also be obtained by multiplying the Process Spin by the difference between the average values of the product sales (ps) and the cost of raw material (rm). The equation is:

**G = w (ps − rm)**

It is therefore concluded that there are two ways to increase Gain. The first is quite obvious: the difference between the selling price and the cost of the raw material is increased, i.e. the product is sold for a higher price and/or a cheaper raw material is obtained. Another way to increase Gain is to accelerate Process Spin, i.e. by evolving the bottleneck Step, according to TOC rules.

Some electronics manufacturers, for example, take advantage of this. They launch ultra-competitively priced products to gain market share and leverage initial sales volume. At first, they practice minimal profit to increase competitiveness and drive competitors away. However, they then initiate optimization rounds that reduce two or more integrated circuits to a single component. Thus, with no need to change the sale price, and due to the cost reduction, the manufacturers get a bigger gain. But the advantages do not stop there. Due to the larger scale of integration, i.e. fewer components to assemble and test, production becomes more agile. If the bottleneck evolves, with process Cyclo spinning faster, the Gain is multiplied again. After a few rounds, the Profits grew a lot and the price remains competitive. It may even go down if the competition comes along.

## *Cyclo Operations*

The previous exercise, in which partners from P&Q Commerce and P&Q Services expanded the P&Q Channel in the country, qualitatively showed the interconnection of Process Cycles. Deepening this analysis from a quantitative point of view, any Step of a given Process can be replaced by a new Cyclo, provided some conditions are met.

Suppose that Cyclo-A, shown at following diagram, is composed of Steps [$S_1$, ... $S_i$, ... $S_n$]. It is not important at the moment to determine Cyclo-A bottleneck or spin. Just consider any Step $S_i$, not necessarily the bottleneck, with Spin equal to Spin($S_i$).

For whatever strategic reason, the Step $S_i$ will be implemented by a partnership interested in putting into practice the philosophy "This is what I can do for you; here's what you can do for me".

All involved agree to use a determined Cyclo as a reference to specify what should be done. Cyclo-B, composed of Steps [$F_1$, ... $F_g$, ... $F_k$], with Step $F_g$ as bottleneck, results in similar processing to Step $S_i$.

What is the impact of this replacement? How to ensure that Cyclo-B replacement will not affect the operation of Cyclo-A?

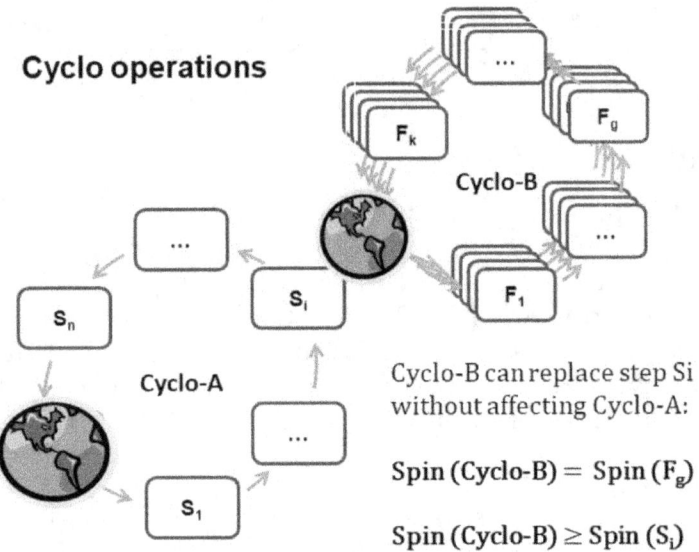

## Cyclo-A
- Steps: [S1, ... Si, ... Sn]
- Bottleneck: Undetermined
- Spin: Undetermined
- Step Si: Processes assets with Spin(Si)

## Cyclo-B  Replaces Step Si of Cyclo-A
- Steps: [F1, ... Fg, ... Fk]
- Bottleneck: Step Fg
- Spin: Spin(Cyclo-B) = Spin(Fg)
- Step Fg: Cyclo-B bottleneck with Spin(Fg)

Note that the Cyclo-B has Spin(Fg), referring to the bottleneck at Step Fg. To ensure that Cyclo-B replacement operation does not affect Cyclo-A, the Spin(Cyclo-B) must be greater than or equal to the original Spin(Si). This ensures that Spin(Cyclo-A) will not be affected by the replacement of Cyclo-B.

# bAmpli: Business Amplifier

So far, the Information System to assist investors and managers in decision-making borrowed and modified the management and manufacturing skills and techniques of the twentieth century, resulting in a process fueled by SPC, JIT, TPM, and TOC.

Steps of the Deming Process, originally queued in open sequence, have been closed in a cycle with the Earth, where it all comes from and where everything returns. Thus, Cyclo's new concept continually spins money and process assets in opposite directions. The speed is the Spin of the bottleneck Step.

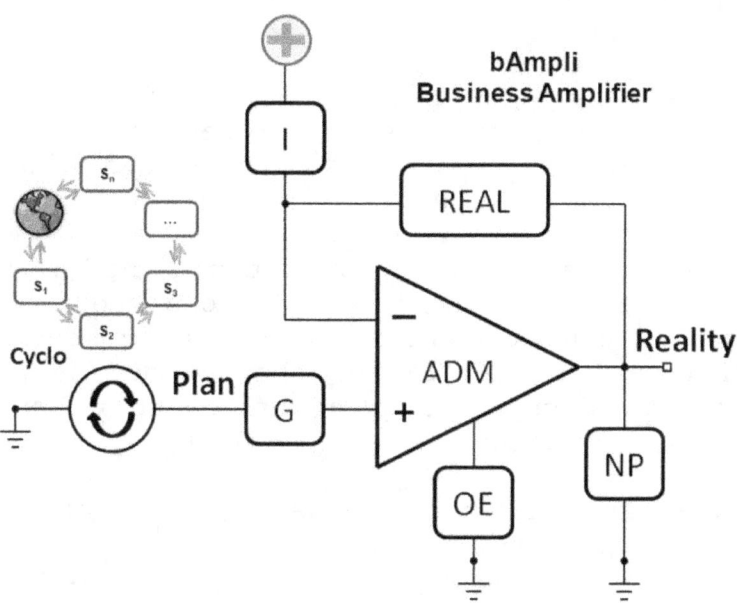

bAmpli, the Business Amplifier powered by a Cyclo, highlights the Plan and Reality, i.e. what you want to do and what is really happening.

The Business Amplifier powered by a Cyclo set up an unprecedented decision-making strategy, with continuous improvement guaranteed through exploration and evolution of process constraints. As a result, investors and managers at every level of the company can, at any time, have a global view of the organization and its role in globalization.

## *Plan x Reality*

The **plan** consists of managing one or more Cyclos that will feed the company's cash with their respective Gains. Equivalent to the power supply of an electronic amplifier, the "+" symbol at the top represents the investor. It feeds the Investment module that backs the business and expects Profit to be rewarded with Return on Investment in a low-risk environment.

In addition to the plan, the Information System captures the naked **reality** of the output, for example, the bank statement with credits and debits in the company's account.

The function of the Administration module is to confront the plan with reality and to promote the action of managers and investors when there are differences. Operating Expense should be fed into to enable the Company to operate and includes Labor and Overhead expenses.

The Administration module has "+" and "-" entries, where the plan and reality feedback come in. Cyclo is considered the plane, so it is connected to the positive input. This is what is expected to happen. If reality confirms the plan, it proceeds in automatic mode.

If there is a disparity between reality and the plan,

action must be taken. If necessary, trigger the investor. When the Gain is negative, for example, to keep Cyclo spinning you will need to inject Investment. This is not expected to happen but it happens.

## bAmpli Gain

By definition, bAmpli's "+" and "-" inputs are considered at the same potential, i.e. if the Gain is positive, both inputs are positive and vice versa. I know it's very little to justify this option, but the equivalent model of an electronic operational amplifier also works that way. Thus, depending on the amount of Gain and the retained Net Profit, we have three possible situations: first a case when Gain is positive. Second, a couple cases may happen in case of negative Gain. Following are the details.

**Positive Gain**

In this case, reality (Real) should confirm that the Net Profit module has accumulated Gain. The confirmation works as if Real has passed resources from the input to the output of the amplifier, as seen in the bAmpli. As an accumulative module, Profit works similarly to the capacitor that accumulates charge in the electronic model. This occurs when you receive more resources from Product Sales than Raw Material payments.

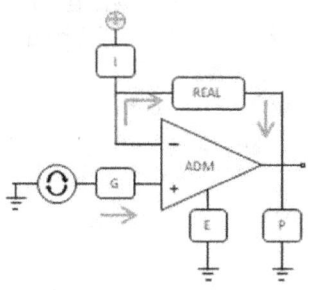

bAmpli operation

G > 0 (accumulates Profit)

## Negative Gain

With negative entries, you need to capture resources. Otherwise, Cyclo runs the risk of "dying", i.e. stop spinning. The investor tries to avoid this as he knows that breaking the inertia to start the machine has a much higher cost. If Real confirms resources accrued in Profit, passes them back from the output to the input of the amplifier. See below that this occurs when there is provision for payment of Raw Material.

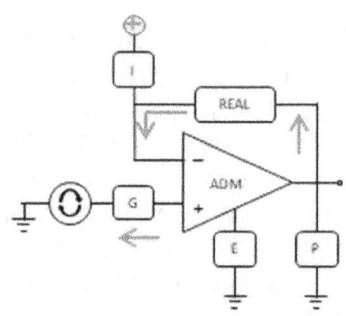

bAmpli operation

G < 0 (with provision)

If there is no accrued provision for the payment of Raw Material to the supplier, the investor must be called upon to release resources through the Investment. Resources must be sufficient to at least clear the Gain. Thus, as shown in the diagram of the Business Amplifier on the left, the debt with the Raw Material supplier is paid off and Cyclo keeps spinning.

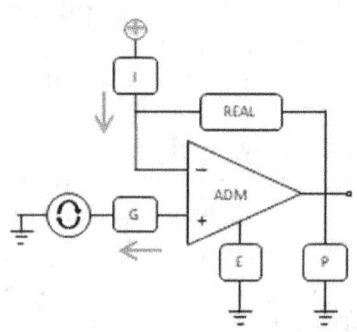

bAmpli operation

G < 0 (no provision)

## *Return on investment*

If all goes as planned, the accumulated gain exceeds the operating expense and generates Net Profit. In this case, the investor is entitled to Return on Investment, with Real returning part of the Net Profit accrued through module I. Then, investor i.e. the "+" at the top, receives funds back. See more details in the diagram shown below.

### bAmpli operation

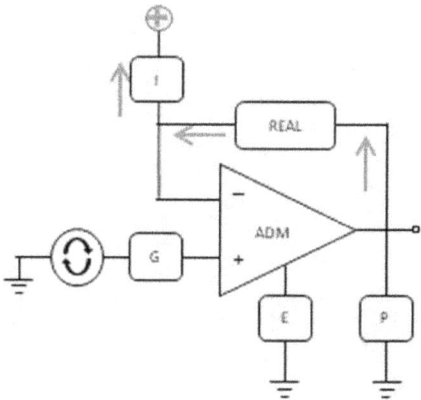

Return on Investment

## Business Circuits

Business Amplifiers can be grouped to form business circuits. In the following example, six separately managed Cyclos contribute together to the same company Profit, as in the case of geographically distributed subsidiaries.

## bAmpli Branches

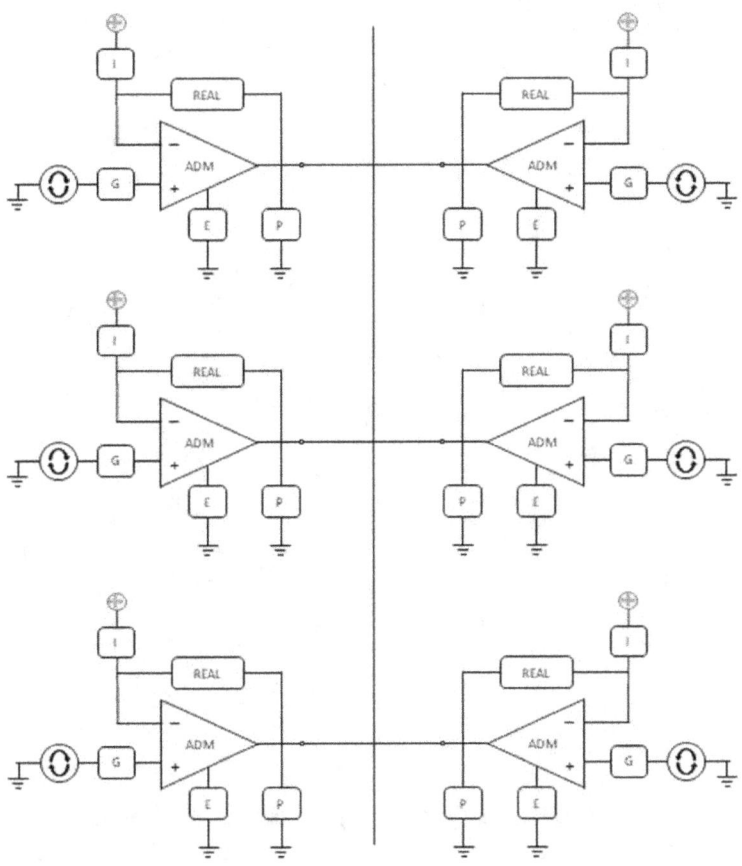

In another example, seen below, the company on the left provides an investment line to leverage three other companies with distinct Cyclos. It can represent an Angel investing resources in Startups, for example.

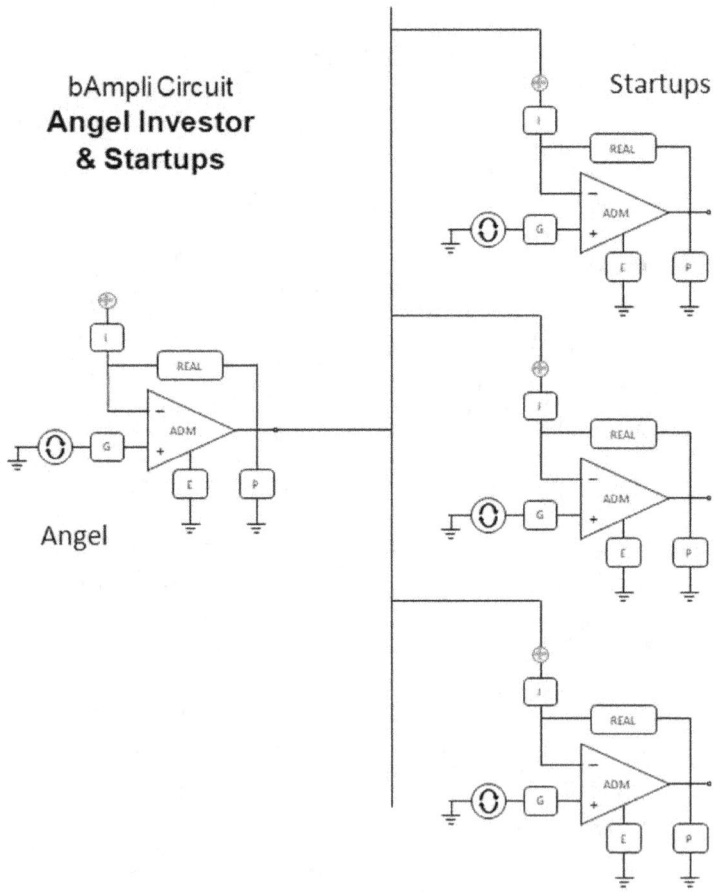

In this case, when the Angel sells its "product", the entire Startup is negotiated, disappearing from the diagram and fattening the Angel's Profit!

# Ampli Business

## *Layers are the solution*

In building the well-established local area network model in the 1970s, tiering equated and laid a solid foundation for dealing with complex communication protocols.

In the ISO/OSI initiative, the International Standards Organization developed the Open Systems Interconnection, a model that played a key role in the design of the Ethernet standard and the Internet itself. One model established operational definitions and standardized the communication functions of a computing system. The IEEE 802.1 working group of the Institute of Electrical and Electronics Engineers is responsible for evolving standards and ensuring network interoperability.

You connect your television to your home theater with a network cable, and an identical cable connects your computer to the Internet router, regardless of model and manufacturer of any of these devices. Even your phone's Wifi electromagnetic waves fit the pattern, connecting you to distant points on the planet. None of this would exist without ISO/OSI initiative.

Goldratt also proposed something like that when he created the Company Indicators. It was a way of establishing a bridge that would serve as a counterpoint to the huge range of Cost Accounting variables. With this, he intended to create a ubiquitous language, understood by all and which would serve as the basis for the evolution of the Theory of Constraints.

To guide investors and managers in their decisions towards the global optimum, an Information System model consisting of simple combined elements that expresses best management and administration practices is needed. With that in mind, and trying to expand exchanges between all companies, the Information System proposes a four-tiered standardization effort:

1. **Company Indicators:** Originating in Cost Accounting, this is the layer with basic financial information of the company. In the middle of the twentieth century, labor became a fixed cost of the company. The Japanese stressed the importance of Return on Investment as a measure of performance;

2. **Cyclo: The Gain Machine** It is based on the original definition of the Deming process, with the additional rule that closes the process cycle with the Earth, where it all comes from and where everything returns. Produces Gain, the most important measure;

3. **bAmpli: Business Amplifier** establishes the rules for Cyclo's administration, redirecting the Gain to the Company's Profit and activating the investor to back the business with Investment;

4. **bAmpli Business Circuit:** The interconnection of Business Amplifiers allows investors and managers to abstract from production Cyclos and focus on the interaction between a group of companies, establishing safe margins for business risk.

Following is a summary of the four proposed layers, consolidating the information and discussions held in previous chapters.

## Layer 1 - Company Indicators

The Company Indicators, listed below, present the basic information to be made available for operations in the upper layers. The simplicity of the equations is vital to their general acceptance and understanding. This is the basic financial information that companies of any type and size should have and maintain.

## Company Indicators

| ------ | Indicator | Description |
|---|---|---|
| RI | Return on Investment | Equals Net Profit divided by Investment; |
| I | Investment | It is all the money the system invests by buying things that the system intends to sell; |
| NP | Net Profit | Product Sales Revenue minus Raw Material, Labor, and Overhead Costs; |
| PS | Product Sales | It is the cash flow received from the sale of products; |
| RM | Raw Material | It is the cash flow that remunerates suppliers; |
| G | Gain | This is the rate at which the system generates money through sales and equals revenue from Product Sales minus Raw Material expenses; |
| WF | Workforce | Company expense with Labor; |
| OH | Overhead | Other fixed costs of the company; |

The following equations reflect the relationships between the Company Indicators:

$$RI = \frac{NP}{I}$$

$$NP = (PS - RM) - (WF + OH)$$

$$G = PS - RM$$

$$OE = WF + OH$$

$$NP = G - OE$$

$$RI = \frac{G - OE}{I}$$

| | |
|---|---|
| RI | Return on Investment |
| I | Investment |
| NP | Net Profit |
| PS | Product Sales |
| RM | Raw Material |
| WF | Workforce |
| OH | Overhead |

## Layer 2 - Cyclo: Gain Machine

Layer 2 defines the Process by Deming's original rules, and the additional Process Cycle rule, where everything leaves Earth and everything returns to Earth.

This also puts into practice Rule Six of the Deming Process which requires that "This is what I can do for you; here is what you can do for me."

Defined in Layer 2, Cyclo generates a cash flow resulting from the difference between Product Sale receipts and Raw Material payments. The Cyclo diagram and the list of rules that define its process are shown below:

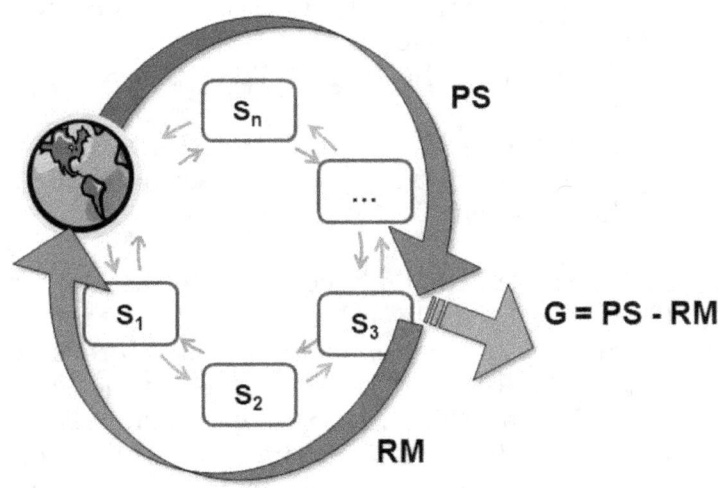

**Cyclo: Gain Machine**

## CYCLO PROCESS

**Step 1 ▶ Step 2 ▶ ... ▶ Consumer**

1. The process is divided into steps;
2. The work enters a Step, changes state, and proceeds with the next Step as a client.
3. At each Stage there is production, that is, something happens in the set of assets that enter a Stage, causing their exit in a different state.
4. Each Step incorporates continual improvement of methods and procedures to meet subsequent Steps.
5. Each Step cooperates with the next and the previous, seeking optimization.
6. The Steps establish long-term trust relationships, such as: this is what I can do for you; here's what you can do for me.
7. The final step is for the consumer, purchaser of the product or service.
8. The steps work together, aiming at quality and customer satisfaction.
9. Consumer is the main link of the production line.
10. The Process is a closed loop that consumes products of nature and transforms them into other products of nature.

The Steps are designed according to the skills and workflow required by the Process. Each Step incorporates a process of continuous improvement, or kaizen. To this end, with the assistance of the SPC, JIT, TPM and TOC, management shall establish operational definitions relating to the Process perform sampling, measurement and construct control charts that assess the quality of production.

If the Process is under statistical control, i.e. free of special causes, the probability distribution of the Step Periods is represented by a normal curve.

Predictable cyclic behavior is expected from the Process, the speed of which is determined by the Process Spin, that is, the inverse of the bottleneck Step Period.

## Layer 3 - bAmpli: Business Amplifier

The bAmpli operation establishes the Layer 3 rules, gauging the plan established by Cyclo and comparing it to the reality of the facts.

Management acts simply and intuitively, channeling Gain to Profit. It can also trigger the Investment to support the business and prevent the "death" of Cyclo, being remunerated by Return on Investment.

Operating Expense is continually fed, covering the Company's fixed costs including Labor and Overhead.

Following is the Cyclo powered Business Amplifier diagram, which highlights:

- the **Plan**: Cyclo is what you want to do;
- **Reality**: The facts, for example, the statement with credits and debits in the company's bank account.

## bAmpli: BUSINESS AMPLIFIER

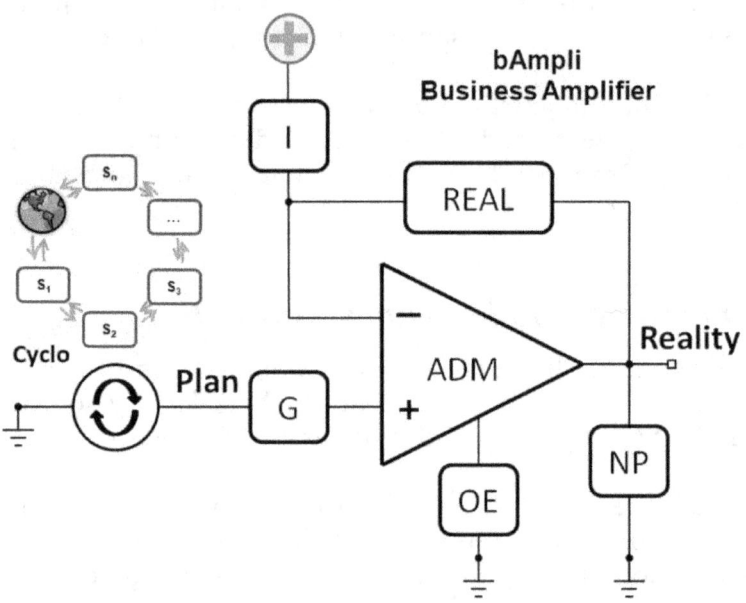

| bAmpli: Business Amplifier ||
|---|---|
| **Cyclo** | Process Cycle that feeds bAmpli with its Gain |
| **Gain (G)** | Difference Between receiving Product Sales and paying Raw Materials |
| **Investor (+)** | Business Owner |
| **Investment (I)** | Money invested in the company |
| **Administration (ADM)** | Company Administration |
| **Reality (REAL)** | Capturing the reality of the facts |
| **Operating Expense (OE)** | Company fixed costs |
| **Net Profit (NP)** | Company net profit |

## Layer 4 - bAmpli Business Circuit

As can be seen below, the Cyclos Diagram accurately expresses the relationship between the parties involved, whether they are under the same shed at the P&Q Factory, or distributed by thousands of Channel P&Q partners in a distant country.

The diagram is flexible and can be expanded indefinitely. Each Cyclo Step can be replaced with a new Cyclo by simply having Spin greater than or equal to the Step to be replaced. Each Cyclo can become a niche, as long as everyone agrees.

Process Cycle Diagram

| | | | | | | | | |
|---|---|---|---|---|---|---|---|---|
| | | $RM → | | | → $PS | | | |
| | | RM ← | | | ← Product | | | |
| Services | User | Project | Proposal | Approval | Purchase | Execution | | Service |
| Commerce | Channel | Logistics | Purchase | Stock | Sales | Marketing | | User |
| Distribution | FOB | Logistics | Purchase | Stock | Sales | Logistics | | Channel |
| Overseas | FOB | Logistics | Importation | Distribution | Commerce | Services | | Service |
| Factory | P-Part | | | | | | | |
| | RM1 | | A | C | | D | | P FOB |
| | RM2 | | B | C | | | | |
| | RM3 | | A | B | | D | | Q FOB |

But only Cyclos, spinning in isolation, doesn't solve the whole problem. They must be connected to their respective bAmpli - Business Amplifiers. Only then can they effectively translate into numbers the expectation that Process Spin offers.

Company Indicators start to flow in bAmpli, through simple and objective operations of the administrative workflow. If the Plan coincides with the Reality of the facts, the operations proceed in automatic mode, freeing human intervention. With this, investors and managers can devote themselves to the noble improvement of Cyclos, i.e. the Process Cycles.

Just looking at the bAmpli Circuit with 4 Cyclos that follows in the next page, it is known that:

- The investor is the "+" at the top left of the circuit;

- The investment is a bAmpli Business Circuit, formed by Cyclos numbered 1 through 4;

- bAmpli from Cyclo 1 invests on Cyclos 2 and 3;

- bAmplis from Cyclos 2 and 3 share their Profit;

- And reinvest it in the Cyclo 4.

Net Profit is expected from these initiatives, providing Return on Investment to investor, i.e. the owner of the bAmpli Circuit, represented by the top "+", to the left of the circuit.

Does the bAmpli 4 Cyclos Circuit remember anything else? See the answer below, following the diagram.

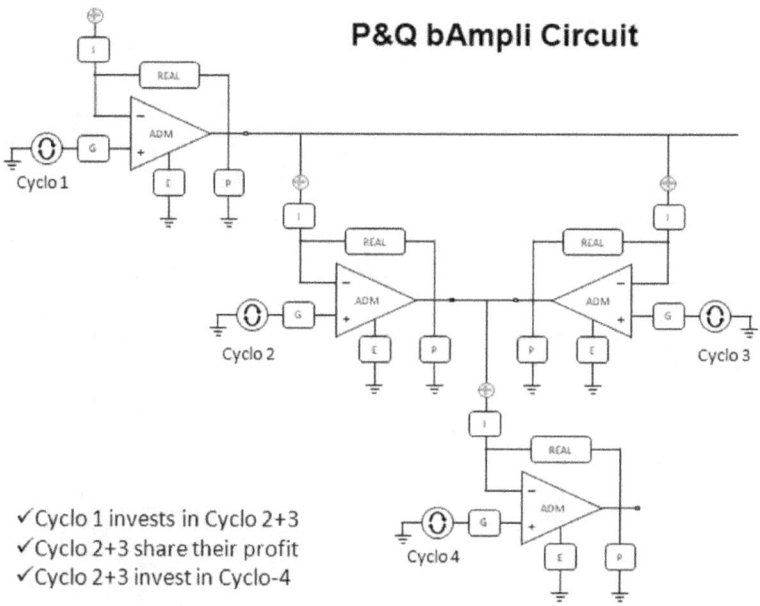

Could Cyclo 1 be the P&Q Factory? Cyclos 2 and 3 are jointly supported, such as P&Q Overseas and P&Q Distribution. Both share their Profit, as their main interest is to promote the P&Q brand in the country. As for Cyclo 4, it can be attributed to any activity that the P&Q group may create in order to delight its customers in the country, keeping Cyclo 1 from the matrix spinning ever stronger!

The bAmpli Business Circuit, result of the association of Business Amplifiers powered by their respective Cyclos, helps investors and managers, at every level of the company, at any time, to have access to the global vision of the organization and its role in globalization.

JOSÉ MOTTA LOPES

# Conclusion

Every 30 years, since the invention of the Ford factory in the '20s, there have been major transformations in business management. Deming in the '50s started the revolution in Asian countries with the SPC, followed by JIT and TPM. In the '80s, Goldratt brought Westerners back to the top with the Theory of Restrictions. It is now important to enhance the information system with continuous improvement towards the global optimum.

To tackle the main current problems head-on, it is necessary to avoid wasting energy by managing conflicts between departments, competing companies, closed countries and continents, and so on. The challenge of creating a business infrastructure that allows the exploration and elevation of bottlenecks would be rewarded by a huge concentration of efforts in the continuous improvement towards the global great.

This proposal presents an Information System organized in layers, which offers an alternative to developing a ubiquitous language to assist investors and managers from companies of all types and sizes, involved in making business decisions.

Our intelligence can be used to make better use of the resources available on Earth. This one is unique. And it belongs to all of us.

# About the author

**José Motta Lopes,** from Rio de Janeiro, graduated in 1977 in Electronic Engineering at UFRJ. In 1982, he obtained an M.Sc degree in the Systems and Computer Engineering Program at COPPE / UFRJ. He worked for ten years as a researcher at CEPEL - Eletrobrás Electric Energy Research Center. During this period, he developed Supervision Centers for Electrical Systems and, in the late 1970s, transferred the design and manufacturing technology of the first generation of PLCs manufactured in the country to the Brazilian industry. In 1985, he founded Mira Informática, a software house that developed a local area network operating system widely used in industrial and office automation. In the 90s, he participated for ten years in the Industrial Data Collection System for SPC at the Quality #1 factory of Ford's Electronic Division in Guarulhos, São Paulo, Brazil. In the 90s, he disclosed Eli Goldratt's Theory of Constraints, through workshops in several cities in Brazil. Then, he served for twenty years as CEO of networking companies in the Brazilian market. Nowadays, he is dedicated to the Internet of Things (IoT) projects and business consulting.

JOSÉ MOTTA LOPES

# Glossary

It follows a succinct definition of selected terms, acronyms and nomenclatures used in this book.

| | |
|---|---|
| bAmpli | *Business Amplifier* powered by Cyclos that establishes an unprecedented decision-making process for managers and investors, with continuous improvement guaranteed through the exploration and evolution of process restrictions. |
| CEO | The *Chief Executive Officer* is the most senior executive in a company. |
| NC | *Numerical Command* is a system developed in the middle of the last century that used perforated tapes to control machines, lathes and machining centers. |
| Cyclo | Gain Machine based on the Process Cycle that generates a cash flow, resulting from the differences between the receipts from the Sale of Products and payments of Raw Materials. |
| Digital PDP-11 | 16-bit minicomputer model, manufactured by Digital in the 70s and 80s. |
| IBM PC/XT/AT | Microcomputer models from the 80s. |

| | |
|---|---|
| IEEE | *Institute of Electrical and Electronic Engineers*, the world's largest technical organization, dedicated to advancing technology for the benefit of humanity, with 420,000 members in 160 countries. |
| IEEE 802.1 | IEEE working group responsible for the evolution and certification of local network standards. |
| ISO | *International Standards Organization.* |
| IoT | Internet of Things. |
| JIT | *Just in Time* is an inventory strategy created at Toyota in the 1960s that revolutionized the industry. It increased efficiency and reduced waste, with the receipt of assets in the production process only when they were needed. |
| kaizen | Unique word in the Japanese language that means "continuous improvement". |
| MRP | *Material Requirements Planning* is a system that planned the material needs of production in the 1960s. |
| MRP II | *Manufacturing Resource Planning* II is a method for planning all the resources of a manufacturing plant in the 1980s. |
| OEM | *Original Equipment Manufacturing* are manufacturers that resell products from other companies under their own name and brand. |

| | |
|---|---|
| OSI | *Open Systems Interconnection*, a layered model from the 70's for the creation of protocols used in local networks. |
| PLC | *Programmable Logic Controller* is a robust industrial computer, used to control industrial and manufacturing processes. |
| PM | *Preventive Maintenance,* used in '70s. |
| ppm | Measure that represents one part per million, that is, 1 ppm is equivalent to 0.0001%. |
| SKU | *Stock Keeping* Unit is a product or service identification code used to track items in an inventory. |
| SPC | *Statistical Process Control.* |
| Spin | It is the number of times that a phenomenon occurs in a certain unit of time. In the case of the Process Cycle, it refers to occurrences during the Working Time. |
| TOC | *Theory of Constraints*, created by Eli Goldratt in the 80s. |
| TPM | *Total Productive Maintenance*, evolution of Productive Maintenance, created by Seiichi Nakajima in the 1970s. |
| VAR | *Value Added Reseller*, a type of reseller that adds the provision of its own service to the products it resells, acting as an integrator. |

JOSÉ MOTTA LOPES

# Bibliography

- Henry Ford, **MY LIFE AND WORK**, 1922.

- W. Edwards Deming, **OUT OF THE CRISIS**, 1982.

- Seiichi Nakajima, **INTRODUCTION TO TPM**, 1988.

- Eliyahu M. Goldratt and Robert E. Fox, **THE RACE**, 1986.

- Eliyahu M. Goldratt, **THE HAYSTACK SYNDROME**, 1991.

JOSÉ MOTTA LOPES

www.ingramcontent.com/pod-product-compliance
Lightning Source LLC
Chambersburg PA
CBHW071411210526
45465CB00001B/340